A Testimony

The TREASURE IN MY HEART

Helena Schwachheim

WinePress Publishing
MUKILTEO, WA 98275

The Treasure in my Heart

Published by:
WinePress Publishing
PO Box 1406
Mukilteo, WA 98275

Cover by **DENHAM**DESIGN, Everett, WA

Except where noted, all Scripture verses are from the King James version of the Bible.

Printed in the United States of America

ISBN 1-57921-025-2
Library of Congress Catalog Card Number: 97-60735

DEDICATED

TO OTHER HEARTS

YEARNING FOR REALITY

I want to express my deep appreciation to Jeanne Poole for the many precious hours spent in editing and to the brothers and sisters in Christ who encouraged me to write and helped in the proof reading: Ed and Tatiana Senechal, Michael Eskew, Susanne Short, Ann Bond, Lynn Bogosian, Sue Atchison, and others.

To His glory!

Helena

Table of Contents

Part I

Part II

Preface

The Treasure in my Heart tells of a vibrant search for the meaning of life. Come with Helena as she retraces significant episodes extending from her early childhood in a family of Russian nobility through the horror of revolution, the flight for their lives, and the years of deprivation in Europe with no real home, to her "making it" in the United States and ultimately obtaining riches beyond the greatest material wealth. Her encounters with the Lord and the ensuing inner response to the Bible are described in a fresh, experiential way. Her life begins to change from the inside out, and she embarks on fascinating adventures as she learns to follow the Lord. Once you start to read this captivating, true story, you won't want to put it down.

A friend,
Ann Bond

In 1968, I was pleading with the Lord to show me the deeper truths in His Word. When Helena came all the way to Vancouver Island and the countryside where I lived. From the first moment I felt Helena's regal inner being and it struck a chord in me. "At last," I said, "this is God's child coming to lead me into the reality of His deeper truths." Helena was the bearer of good tidings with great joy!

Mother of nine,
Phyllis Mattingsley

What *Pilgrim's Progress* alluded to concerning a spiritual journey, this book shines clearly for all to see in practice and in reality. The key to survival in a violent world is delicately unveiled as we follow a seemingly lone girl on her expedition in pursuit of the ultimate treasure.

Young Peoples' co-worker,
Edward Steven Senechal

Every child truly born of God has a unique story to tell of his calling and salvation. Not many have put their story on paper. This is one that should be told.

God chose to reveal Himself to Helena. What appears to be accident and tragedy is only part of many steps to her transformation. We hope that each reader will be truly touched and genuinely enriched by Helena's experiences.

Jeanne Poole M.D.
Jeffrey Poole, Attorney at Law

Part I

1

My Legacy

I was born in November of 1915, in the southern Russian city of Odessa, during a most turbulent time in European and Russian history. World War I was raging. Most Russian able-bodied men, along with my father, were conscripted into the army. When the Bolsheviks entered St. Petersburg to overthrow the Czarist government in October 1917, they took advantage of the scarcity of adult men at home. A bloody massacre followed in St. Petersburg and quickly erupted all over Russia. The revolutionary fighting did not reach the south of Russia until at least a year later.

If Only We Had Listened

From my early childhood, I had an inner, unspoken and inexplicable, sense of dignity, nobility, and happiness. It was just a *joie de vivre!* I was unable to share this with anyone. It was a sense which was in total opposition to my outer circumstances and to my behavior. This *something* was present deep in my being and occasionally came to the surface in the most unusual ways.

The first instance of unusual behavior, later related to me by my mother, occurred in the year 1918 when I was three years old. The Bolsheviks had come to Odessa ransacking, pillaging, and killing.

In the early years of the revolution, our family had felt secure in their French townhouse built of hewn rock. Although the ground floor windows had been barricaded, and in spite of being in the care of my nanny and other household help, I somehow managed to sneak out of the house. I would walk around nearby streets and discover the horrible results of the war. For years, I recalled the sight of dead men hanging from lampposts and dead horses in the streets. Mother said that I would go to the horses, hold their heads, and try to resuscitate them. When my efforts were clearly to no avail, I would run home terrified.

There was a short time of respite from the fighting when the White Army repelled the Red Army. Things quieted down; however, the war-destructive images could not leave me and I wanted to escape. Mother said that I continually pleaded with her and the relatives in the house. “Let us go; let us get out; let us leave, take everything with us...please don’t forget me. Mama, don’t forget me.” There was such persistence and alarm in my voice that I bothered everyone again and again.

“I wish we had listened to you,” My mother was to later say. “If only we had listened, there would not have been such immense difficulties and years of suffering in poverty and exile. If only we had listened.”

My Family

On my father’s side was Baron Yagor von Schwachheim, a landowner near the city of Nikolaiev, northeast of Odessa. He was a descendant of a Minister and Superintendent of Agriculture to the Court of Bavaria in Munich, Germany, who had been invited by Katherine the Great to homestead and develop the agriculture in southern Russia. The family prospered. My grandfather built cheese factories in Nikolaiev and Kishinev to put the milk of his cattle herds to good use.

Grandfather was married to Elena Dimitrenko, who was from a wealthy middle class family. His aunts were rather arrogant old women who spoke French all the time and were not at all happy with his engagement. They already had a rich daughter from the peerage in mind. But Grandfather was determined and forced their blessing. They had three children: my Aunt Olga, my uncle Volodya, and my father Serge.

Very recently I received a telephone call from a great niece, Tatiana Marcotty, the granddaughter of my uncle Volodya, of whom I had never heard, and she mailed me a short and incomplete biography of Aunt Olga. Tatiana gave me the liberty of using a few extracts. Aunt Olga writes:

"Our family was made up of Papa, Mama, myself as the oldest, Volodya and Seryoja (Serge), and our nearest help: Nyanya, Madame Lina (until my tenth year) then Klärchen or Fraulein Notz from Munich. We lived close together. It was a life full of love and understanding. Never a misunderstanding or quarrel, ever. To educate us was their noble work. It was totally unthinkable for us to ever say something mean or untrue.

"We loved our father very much. How full of happiness their marriage was! People keep on looking for happiness in luxury and fame and pass right by that which is often so close. Happiness is where love blossoms. But love has been made into a joke and children are being born now to whom such happiness cannot be given any more and children's fine feelings are not respected enough. I was very fortunate to have had a childhood built on love and respect of the parents for one another. We were not spoiled, but our young souls were not insulted nor crushed by anything. Neither by words nor deeds. A noble and clean life was reflected in the relationship of the parents.

"In spite of his wealth my dearest father was an extremely modest man who never desired much for himself. The first years of their married life they lived on his family's huge estate of Voyevodskoye, but in a very old house in primitive surroundings and no modern comfort. The rooms were low and dark because the house was surrounded by big old trees. The furnishings were still from the days of the great-great grandfathers–a lot of large sofas standing in the living rooms for people to sleep on overnight during

board meeting days. Those people were controllers and administrators of the estate and were employed by the Baron.

"Around 1897, Papa and Mama decided to build themseleves a new comfortable house. We were almost grown up and the old house of Voyevodskoye had grown too small. There were several plans, either to build a new house or buy another estate with a house. After some deliberation, Papa asked Nyanya, the nannie, 'Well, what do you think? Shall we sell Voyevodskoe or shall we buy a new house?'

'But it is unthinkable to leave Voyevodskoe, Yagor Yagorovich, it is your homeland.' The decision was made, the house would be built on the estate.

"Papa commissioned a famous architect, Mr. Duvern. He was to look for the most favorable place for the house, using part of the unused garden. A lot of earth had to be moved. Many masters came from abroad, electrical engineers and a fountain master for the artesian well. At that time it was not easy to organize. I remember exactly the day Mr. Duvern arrived and we all accompanied him on his inspection of the garden. 'Dear Baron, you want to build a house here, here in these woods next to the old house? We will have to build three terraces. The house with the drive will stand on the middle terrace, the upper terrace will hold the tennis court and the French fruit garden; there will be a great stairway to the lowest terrace holding the fountain and the rose garden. The whole thing will take three years.' Papa contributed a great deal to these plans and let his fantasy roam free.

"For the garden, a skilled gardener who grew trees was brought from Germany to start a tree nursery. There was another gardener busy in the orangery who cared for the flowers. Another one, Paul, was responsible for the vegetables; he grew asparagus to be sent all over Russia. Every spring when we came back to the estate we didn't recognize it; everything was new. The barns, the stables and the tool sheds were new. A gigantic silo had risen (the first in Russia). The buildings were far apart and formed several courts framed by bushes. The old buttery was turned into a dairy with large cellars

for cheese storage. We produced mostly Dutch cheese. So, most of the works of planning and implementation were done by Papa. He was loved and respected by all. Many university people came to see this model estate. Many friends came to inspect. A new life began."

I remember seeing photographs of his estate. It was a jewel of a mansion with beautiful rose gardens and terraces with marble balustrades. Marble was easy to clean and considered germ free, so it was also used in the stables of his prize horses, which he raised for the royal houses of Europe. I was told he was an unusual man who would go into the woods alone to his *isba* and remain there for as long as three weeks at a time. He was seventy-two when he was constrained to leave his estate as the Red Army was advancing. He went with grandmother to Sebastopol and rented an apartment there. Sebastopol was a naval port and became an evacuation port for many of the refugees and the nobility in the south of Russia. One afternoon grandfather said that he was very tired, and he laid down on the couch. Grandmother sat by his side. He said again that he was very tired. There was a hush in the room and he said, "He has come for me. The Lord has come for me." He rose up, kissed grandmother good-bye, and laid back with his head on grandmother's lap. He was gone with a smile. This was in 1919.

My father, Baron Serge von Schwachheim, who had been drafted and sent to the European Eastern Front, came home after the war in 1918, only to divorce my mother. This was a great shame to the family. My mother was devastated, I was told. Although I had just turned three years old, I have no recollection of my father. He had simply abandoned us. Aunt Olga's biography gave me some insight and understanding of his irresponsibile disposition. She writes,

"...from childhood on, he was fascinated by machines, often he was found in the mill, or the shop or with horses. Everywhere he joined in the work and came home filthy. His linen suits had to be changed three times a day. The whole time one heard: 'Seryoja! Go and wash your hands and change your suit!' He was the parents'

darling and was frightfully spoiled. This was because of his severe illnesses, when he hung between life and death for four months and we lived the entire summer in danger of losing him. Scarlet fever, diphtheria and dysentery had totally altered him."

Indeed his character reflected none of the kindness, responsibility and nobility of the family and had a tragic effect on my life and mother's.

This family sketch would not be complete without remembering a score of faithful and dedicated servants. Aside from Nyanya and Klärchen there were:

"Fyodor the coachman with his darling horses. Before reaching the driveway he would crack the whip to drive up in style. Before the drive stood the manager-steward, the housekeeper and the gardner with flowers.

"Our village was surrounded by the deepest solitude. The peasants who lived there had once been our body-owned serfs of whom several were still alive. Their leader was Babooshka Tatiana, as we used to call her. She was still our laundress and was proud to have been washing our laundry for three generations. What I knew from past generations I had gleaned from the memories of our former serfs, mainly from Babooshka Tatiana. I would sneak in on her in the washhouse, especially during ironing week. She told me that Papa was two years old when his mother died in Florence, Italy, where he was born. His father died soon after. Yagor von Schwachheim was an orphan at the age of two! He was raised by his mother's sisters among princes and princesses."

There is much more to the biography, even showing more of the ambiance and character of the family. Aunt Olga continues:

"I must also mention our servant in chief, Andreas, who worked for us for years and was totally a member of our family. At the end, he became very familiar, greeted our guests as they arrived and once said to one of our friends who had not visited from some time, 'His excellency has grown old!' He did get a reprimand for that! There was a chamber maid, a seamstress, a cook and many other servants."

On my mother's side of the family was Baron Michel Rainaud, at one time a marshall of the nobility in the south of Russia (which gave him the privilege of endorsing the Czar's expenses while the Czar and his entourage visited the south). He was a member of the Russian *Duma* (parliament) in St. Petersburg and president of the Russian World Bank and had a dozen other distinctions. He was a true statesman, a noble and valiant man, who had given hospitality to three of the White Army generals: Denikin, Koltchak, and Wrangel, at one time or another during the Revolution. He was a man who chose exile, losing his honor, his fortune, his estate, and his citizenship, rather than submit to the Communists. He remained in his homeland until General Wrangel's last stand in November of 1920. He mourned the loss of his country until his death in 1935, dying somewhere in Yugoslavia, poor, forgotten, with only his wife by his side. My grandmother Elena Artyouhova had four children: two sons, my uncles Theodore and Michel, and two daughters, Hélène, my mother, and Tatiana.

During his life, my grandfather Baron Michel Rainaud had been very interested in United States history and government. Before World War I, he drove a big Ford convertible. At the *Duma* there had been an attempt to write a governing document to form a constitutional monarchy, steering away from the autocratic government of the Czar. He had the foresight to see that a democracy could not yet work. The majority of the Russian people were factory workers and peasants, uneducated, and not yet prepared for self-government. Democracy was a concept foreign to most. Today we are witnessing in Russia a painful and disastrous manifestation of such a thoughtless and reckless move, without transition, from autocratic communism to democracy. What democracy? Democracy needs an educated, moral, and spiritually enlightened citizenry. We in the United States today are losing our moral foundations; most Russians never had them.

Apart from his townhouse in Odessa, Grandfather Rainaud had a summer home, Cape Cod style, on his large estate by the

Boog River northeast of Odessa. It took a man on horseback an entire day to encircle his land, most of which was in pasture (the Russian steppes), for his herds of cattle. The grass grew tall enough to hide a rider and his horse.

The whole village worked for grandfather. Money was scarce among the peasants, but every family had their *isba*, which is a log cabin, a milking cow; chickens, rabbits, sheep, goats, or geese. There were a few horses.

My grandfather was kind and he cared for his villagers. He built them a one-room school house and my mother offered to teach the children reading, writing, and arithmetic. Very few children would show up voluntarily. Mother had to go through the village to round them up because the parents were not at all cooperative. "Our folks do not read. *We* do not read. Why do the children have to?" Their excuses were quite valid. The little boys gathered eggs and cleaned the chicken coops; the older ones took the cows to pasture or herded the sheep and goats. The girls cared for the younger children and tended the vegetable garden. Indeed, the chores were plentiful. Besides, this was their way of life, and they were too stubborn to change. Eventually, my mother had to give up trying to teach.

In the *summer of 1918*, when the first commissar came to incite the villagers against my grandfather, quite a few peasants came to the iron gate of the estate, which was some hundred feet from the house. They came with pitchforks, shovels, rakes, and pipes, led by the Communist agitator. My grandfather came out on the porch, standing all of five feet five inches tall. He was not intimidated. "What is wrong?" (He knew very well.) "What has happened? Are your families sick?" He called them by name: "Sasha, Anatoli, Petia, Boris—you had better go back to work in the fields." Sheepishly, they turned around and left. The commissar, defeated, left altogether.

His home town, Odessa, had been a free city during the time of the Duke of Richelieu of France. My great-great grandfather, Chevalier Jean Rainaud, had been an architect under the noted Baron Haussmann in the city of Paris. My mother did not know about this, but on the Quais of the River Seine in Paris, where vendors sell old books, there was a buttress with wooden boxes full of books. Browsing amongst these books one day, my mother found one on Parisian architects, and there was a paragraph about Chevalier Jean Rainaud, who was called to Odessa by Katherine the Great to plan the rebuilding of the city similar to the plans used in Paris. He had been one of the architects working with Haussmann, who built the Place de l'Étoile as a hub with twelve main avenues in all directions, large avenues like the Champs Elysées with several rows of trees. Odessa, being on the seashore, allowed for only half a hub with the statue of Richelieu in the center. This is why Odessa had a French flavor. It explains many of the remaining sites, such as the Great Stairway and the Opera House. The boulevard along the sea was called the Boulevard Français before the Revolution. Today it is the *Nabirejne*, which means "on the Sea Shore." As commendation for his work, Chevalier Jean Rainaud received the title of Baron.

Aunt Olga gives us gives additional details:

"On the north shore of the Black Sea lies Odessa. It was founded by Katherine the Great, who had a harbour built there. The site of Odessa is especially beautiful. She commissioned mainly foreigners with the architecture, Chevalier Jean Rainaud being one of the architects, who created wonderful streets, buildings and gardens. The two principal implementers of her plans were Count Langeron de Ribasse and the Duc de Richelieu. Roads and streets were named after them and the aristocrats built their palaces along the great boulevard. It was one of the most beautiful streets in the world. On one side of the boulevards there were parks and gardens, on the other, restaurants, palaces, and hotels, as well as two memorials. Majestic, broad stairs came up from the harbour to end in a square. In the morning, children went for walks there with their nurses or governesses until about noon. Then there was a cannon shot. The cannon, which was a Turkish spoil, stood next to the Council House and was aimed at the sea.

"Between 2 and 3 o'clock, the street picture changed. Ladies went out for drives in their carriages on the asphalt streets. Asphalt was still a rarity at the turn of the century. One turned around at the Vorontzov palace and stayed in the main square for a while. The public enjoyed the view and made conversation. Music was played on the boulevards and the coffee houses were bursting. At the other end of the boulevard was the theater, the pride of the city. Its fame was not in vain. The Paris and Vienna opera houses are richer, but the position, the acoustics and comfort of the Odessa opera house were unsurpassed.

"The streets in Odessa are very wide and lined with acacia trees. In May, during the time of acacia blossoms, the whole city is perfumed. The climate is most pleasant, temperate and mild in winter, and the summers are hot. The privileged went to their dachas. *But this was not only for the wealthy. Many, many people had gardens and summer houses by the Black Sea.*

"The city was very wealthy and grew very fast. During my youth [writes aunt Olga who was born in 1882] *there were about 600,000 people, mostly Greeks, Italians, Germans and Jews. Many Frenchmen as well. The city's layout was especially favorable to trade: it was a free port, namely a free trade area.... As time passed it became more advantageous to plow the steppes and grow wheat, oats, corn, as well as beets. All this produce was shipped to Odessa and sent to many countries in the world, especially by the Italians who became rich very fast. The second generation of these business men were often multi-millionaires."*

Between October 1917 and 1919, Grandfather Rainaud had scraped together about fourteen million rubles in large denominations from different assets, foreign currencies, and investments he had had in the international market, which currencies he converted into rubles for patriotic reasons. He resented the other countries, particularly Germany and Great Britain, for allowing the Communists to invade Russia. The Russian ruble was worth fifty American cents in 1920. It had taken my grandfather a couple of years to convert some of the family assets into cash, and now overnight he was left with a suitcase of worthless paper. The ruble was not only devalued but also reprinted with Lenin's picture on it. This left the entire family–uncles, cousins, wives, children–destitute because my grandfather was the patriarch of the family.

Much later in life I understood something about my grandfathers. Here were two barons, both endowed with fame, fortune, and social prominence, having the same lifestyle, outwardly fitting the same image of wealth. The similarity ended on the day of their deaths. One died peaceably, still in his homeland, with his head on his wife's lap, looking joyfully into eternity. There was no suffering, no pain. He escaped exile. "*O death, where is thy sting? 0 grave, where is thy victory*?" The other died in exile, though courageously, in poverty, in sickness, with no family at his side, beside his wife, and only a flicker of belief in Christ. What a difference there was between these two deaths! And what was the difference? Was it coincidence? No! There was a drastic difference in faith.

Oh, Lord! Remember Your promise in John 3:16, "*For God so loved the world, that He gave His only begotten Son, that whosoever believeth in Him should not perish, but have everlasting life.*" Grandfather Michel believed in Christ, but only in a formal way. I can only hope he was truly saved and received everlasting life.

Grandfather Schwachheim believed and experienced the reality of a living God. His life reflected Him. He must have responded to an inner sense and sought God, particularly during those peaceful, unexplained retreats into the woods. The Lord's coming to him at his death confirmed his prior experience of the Lord. He knew and believed in Him. He had faith; he had a Treasure in his vessel. He surely passed it on to me. "*We have this Treasure in earthen vessels.*"

In retrospect, I can see this eternal Treasure was there throughout my life. I always believed in God, and subconsciously often listened to an inner prompting. All these events made a lasting impression on me at an early age. Consciously or subconsciously, neither fame, fortune, nor position ever took hold of me because I had seen them vanish in a fleeting moment. I am still very unimpressed by and indifferent to money. All was futile and fickle. "*All is vanity under the sun*," says the preacher. Although my earthly inheritance was lost, the deep sense of dignity, nobility and happiness remained.

This spiritual awareness was my legacy, my rich heritage, a hidden Treasure in my life, which this book will attempt to follow in its growth and maturity. "*Thus saith the Lord that made thee, and formed thee from the womb, which will help thee.*" So that I may know "*that the excellency of the power may be of God, and not of us.*"

2

Years of Survival: Hungary

From Russia to Hungary

If only we had listened, a little child would have led the entire family out of disaster. God often speaks to little children. He spoke to Samuel in the Old Testament. Adults—learn to listen to little children; you could be hearing the voice of God. Do not despise them. "*...Suffer little children, and forbid them not to come unto me; for of such is the kingdom of heaven.*"

Never underestimate the comprehension of a child. The child might not be able to express his feelings, but something within is comparing, sorting, recording, and piling up data for future reference and reaction. So much is learned by the age of five. It is known that a child of that age has mastered the structure of his mother tongue. Only the vocabulary keeps growing as the general knowledge increases.

If only we had listened, there would not have been a hurried flight two years later to Constantinople out of Sebastopol on a Russian ship. We fled with barely a few clothes, jewelry, and fur coats. We remained in Constantinople for six months. Several members of my mother's family stayed together: my uncle Michel, his wife and son; my uncle Theodore and his wife with two daughters; and a second cousin, Serge, with his wife and two children. There were six children in all, ages three to six.

I vividly remember the little donkeys at St. Sofia Square, who had beautiful harnesses with red, yellow, and green pompons and little bells. Once in awhile we were able to ride those donkeys. Although we did not always have the money, we went there every day to check up on them. I also remember trying to iron a shirt for my uncle when no one was looking. I left the old-fashioned iron, heated by coals, sitting on the shirt and burnt a hole in it. The entire household was exasperated with me.

While in Constantinople, my cousins and I went exploring through town. My six-year-old cousin knew his way around immediately. No one ever got lost. Of course, at the same time we became familiar with the Turkish language, and therefore we were the ones who bought food and helped our parents sell some jewelry. We were their official interpreters. All that the adults knew how to say was "*Inch-Allah*" and "*Shalom aleichum*,"—and that is all I remember today. You touch your forehead, your heart, and your mouth, and then you take a bow while you are saying, *Shalom aleichum*! Peace be with you.

It was in Constantinople that General Wrangel came aboard a destroyer which housed the remaining high command of the Russian White Army. When all was lost, the destroyer left Russian waters, and my mother and I were invited to go along. We all were hoping to land in France. Our coming aboard would later prove to be the men's salvation because for six months no country around the Mediterranean Sea would allow them to land due to the devastation from the war and the inability of the nations to absorb thc immigration from Russia. All provisions were sent to the ship by small craft upon the request of the flagman. No one wanted us because the mood of the day was "Hail Communism" and "Down with Men of Valor."

When the destroyer reached the shores of Italy again, the men conceived a plan to let my mother and me go with the gondoliers who came to serenade the ships in Venice. They knew these romantic gondoliers would appreciate her noble appearance and would be flattered to row her ashore. Of course, I had to go along too, and no sooner had I stepped out of the gondola than I ran toward some sailors and started hugging them, to the utter dismay of my mother. One sailor picked me up and my mother had to tear me out of his arms while I was adding embarrassment to her dismay. Subconsciously, I must have been looking for a father. Fortunately, we were on Piazza San Marco, and the hundreds of pigeons provided another distraction to the exuberance of a five year old.

From Venice my mother was to contact some White Russians on the French Riviera on their property in Hyères, which had been their winter resort and had become a gathering place for a few displaced noblemen. General Wrangel asked them for a rendezvous at sea. They were to bring all available sea craft, from yachts to row boats to canoes, to a very specific point of latitude and longitude, at a precise hour under the cover of the darkness of the new moon. This mission was accomplished. I do not know what happened to the destroyer, but afterward, my mother and I were left alone in Venice. She knew very little Italian, only what she had learned from operatic arias. The question was, *where* would we go from here?

After my paternal grandfather's death in Sebastopol in 1919, my grandmother left for Vienna where she had friends and a little money. It was enough to give her a monthly income for some time, enough for food. From Venice, my mother contacted my grandmother in Vienna and we traveled there by train. This was an uncertain step, which had to be followed up quickly by another, because we could not become a burden to grandmother and her daughter, my aunt Olga.

On the Farm

Budapest was not far away, and a family friend, Baron A. Weiss, lived there. He was the owner of the Czepel armament works. The Weiss family supplied arms to the Austro-Hungarian empire. Later, after the dissolution of that empire, they supplied Hungary and other nations with arms. Baron Weiss received not only mother and me, offering us the use of their farm, but also my mother's two brothers and one of her cousins. The country reminded my mother's brothers of the Russian steppes, where cattle could roam, graze and multiply, making their owners a fortune. Together my uncles came up with an idea. They collected their jewelry and fur coats and sold them in town. They collected enough money to buy a herd of twenty-seven cows. I vividly remember the drive home, sitting on the neck of the leader and holding on to her horns. Everyone was filled with hope and expectation of better days to come, but alas, it lasted only for a week. The cows had developed hoof-and-mouth disease, which the buyers could not detect at the time of purchase. The Hungarian peasants had easily outwitted them. Once again, our small family was destitute. What a sad tragedy! Yes, they had been landowners with abundant cattle on their estates, but none of them had ever come near a cow.

However, they did know about horses. They were all experienced horsemen, including mother. Once, Mother had injured her back falling off a horse on my paternal grandfather's estate. It was amazing that she recovered. She was not warned ahead of time that she had mounted a very spirited horse, a jumper, which is much different from a race horse. The corrals for these horses were six feet tall and were intended to keep the jumpers in. She no sooner mounted him in the corral than he took off toward a six foot fence. It all happened in a flash. Mother realized that he was going to jump and tried to hold him back, but he was not about to slow down. He jumped, and mother was thrown out of the saddle. Mother was a very good jumper, but the horse did not have enough momentum to completely clear the six foot fence. The fall was tremendous, and although seriously bruised, she recovered without any permanent injury. The Invisible ONE spared her for me!

On the farm, there were beautiful horses to whom I could feed a handful of hay or a carrot. I would stand in front of one, shake my head and he would shake his in return. "Oh," I thought, "it must be fun to ride on one of them like my uncles did." And try I did. To everyone's astonishment and fear they watched me galloping away, bareback, hanging onto the racer's mane. We were free, flying in the wind, through fields and roads and prairies, both of us.

The adults, on the other hand, worried, "What if the prize horse breaks a leg? What if she falls off?" Those adults always worry about something that might happen and doesn't.

I do not remember getting a spanking, which I really did not need as my rear end was already raw from the ride, but I was severely talked to and the stables were off limits from then on. This did not dampen my spirit very long. I turned to other smaller animals: my rabbit, the puppy, and my friend, the porcupine.

My rabbit: No longer allowed to spend my play time with horses, I went around the farm buildings to see what I could find, and to my great surprise and delight I found a white rabbit in a cage about three feet off the ground at just the right height for me. He was so beautiful, white as snow with brilliant red eyes. His long ears stood straight up when he saw me come, and he hopped to the front of the cage. We greeted one another with joy. He was lonely and I was lonely. He wanted to play and I wanted to play. I put my fingers through the wire of the cage, and he let me scratch his head.

He had a funny, little nose so soft and pink that twitched and sniffed all the time. But, it was his ears that did the talking. The ears were lying down when the rabbit was tired; they went straight up when he was excited or interested, or one ear up and one down when nothing was going on. He was always on the alert. Often, being all alone and caged in, he was sad, and I was sad, having no one to play with. We became pals, understanding one another instinctively. I would tell stories to my rabbit, and he would listen. Sometimes I could bring him a treat, a piece of carrot or a slice of cabbage. There was no fresh grass since it was still winter, and I was not allowed to let him out of the cage. I loved my little rabbit. He was my friend, my pal. He was mine!

Early that spring, mother made me a pink dress out of her silk taffeta petticoat brought from Russia. It was for a special occasion. We had been invited by the Weiss family to spend a couple of days with them in Budapest. They had two girls about my age. "You must bring them a present," said mother.

"But I do not have anything." True, I did not have a single toy.

"Yes, you do. You have a rabbit. You bring them your rabbit." The words fell like a block of ice into my heart. I froze.

"Mama, he is my only friend. I cannot give him away!"

"Yes, you can. You must learn to share." I was numb.

I do not remember how we arrived in Budapest nor how I gave away my rabbit. My hurt for my lost friend remained buried in my heart for years. I was worried not so much about giving him away as I was for his well-being. The girls were city girls. They had a closet full of dead dolls and stuffed animals without life. How would they know how to care for a live rabbit? What would they do with him? Could they make him happy? Where would he live? Back on the farm, I mourned him for days. Mother's attempts to reassure me were little solace. How could I go on living without my pal?

The puppy: A friend of the family, concerned for me, tried to fill the void my rabbit had left with a new distraction. He came one afternoon and told me, "Put your hand in my coat pocket." There was a living and warm bundle of fur in it. I pulled out a little white doggie with brown and black spots. "It's a fox terrier," said Mama. He was so wiggly I could not hold him. On the ground he would run round and round in circles and then run away. Never could he stay still long enough to be talked to like I had talked with my rabbit. I wanted to tell him fairy tales, but he was not interested and ran away. Somebody had cut off his tail. Maybe that was why he was so jumpy. I did not know why, except that he never became a close pal.

By the end of the summer the puppy was almost full grown but still just as wiggly and jumpy. "Go and tie that dog to a tree," ordered Mother. I had never seen a dog tied to a tree.

"How am I going to do that?" I caught the doggie by the collar, for he did have some sort of a collar. Then I found a rope and pulled him to a small tree. Standing him up on his hind legs, his back against the tree trunk and having attached the rope to his collar, I proceeded to wind the rope around the tree and the dog's belly, round and round. Finding a piece of barbed wire, I secured the job. I was worn out.

When the dog was well tied, I returned to join the adults in the house. "What were you doing so long?" they wondered.

"You told me to tie the dog to the tree. It was a hard job. I do not know how I managed."

The dog started whining and yelping louder and louder, finally attracting the adults' attention who quickly released him from his ordeal. The dog was free, but I was laughed at, feeling humiliated.

My friend, the porcupine: Small, wooded areas were not far from the farm, and I was free to roam them. One afternoon, at the edge of the woods, I met up with a strange little animal. It was smaller than a rabbit. He was very close when I noticed him, but he did not run away. I crouched on my heels and started to talk to him gently. All his fur stood on end. What was that? Coming still closer, I could tell they were prickers. He looked like a prickly ball. Underneath you could see a sweet, little face with shining, beady eyes. He sat there going nowhere, and I also sat down to have a friendly talk with him. We looked at each other, and I assured him that I meant no harm and only wanted to play. He listened. Little by little he lowered his sharp quills and allowed me to reach out and scratch his head. Most animals love to have their heads scratched. After a while, having gained his confidence, he let me pick him up in my arms—easy does it—and I brought him home.

Mother could hardly believe what she saw. "Where did you get this porcupine? However did you manage to pick him up?"

"Oh!" I answered, "so that is a porcupine!" "We need to give him something to eat, some milk and bread, and we have to keep him in our room." I was bossy. After all, I knew better than mother.

"In that case," my mother answered, "you must care for him yourself." As soon as I put the porcupine down, up came his quills, and my new friend quickly hid under the bed. At night he would leave his hiding place to find food. We could hear him thump around the room. On the third day he escaped to go back to his real home, the woods. I was glad he had a home he liked better. To each his own!

After the loss of the herd, the men decided to remain on the farm to help exercise and train the saddle and race horses of Baron Weiss, at least until further developments. They lived from day to day. One by one my uncles left on some uncharted course to France, where my aunts and cousins had gone before. Mother and I stayed behind with the only cow that survived. That cow was not part of the twenty-seven. She was beautiful in her light caramel-colored coat. Her udder was huge, and she gave more milk than any other cow—22 liters a day, which at that time was a lot. Her name was Milje, and she went with us when we moved to the hunting castle.

The Hunting Castle

After my uncles left, the farm house was no longer a proper place for my mother to live, because there were only farm hands there. Our benefactor gave us the use of a little hunting castle on a hill across a valley. It was actually a fortified look-out post built centuries before to fight off the Turks and the Huns. It consisted of the lookout tower, which was now a convenient residence for owls and bats, a large room converted into a ballroom for dances and dinner parties, a few bedrooms, and the kitchen quarters, all of which had been renovated at the turn of the century. It was more or less livable. Owners and friends still used it during the fall hunting season. Since it was built out of stone it was very cold. We had no electricity, no running water, no inside toilets—just like on the farm. We did have kerosene lamps and plenty of firewood, which mother chopped with an ax. Good enough! No one ever complained. It was the lifestyle of many. We were thankful to have a roof over our heads.

We used the kitchen and one bedroom, and I was allowed to play in the ballroom. We had had a real ballroom in the house in Odessa, which was converted into a playroom for me and my five cousins when the street fighting was raging. Here in this fort, however, everything was peaceful.

The rest of the place and the tower were off-limits. They had been left to the owls, the bats, and the rats. Rats! Mother was at constant war with rats. She fought them off with poison at night. In the morning she quickly went to collect the dead rats not only for health reasons but to keep me from playing with them. I was only seven. Such plump and furry little creatures made good make-believe horses. I harnessed them, six of them, with strings and things to a make-believe carriage. A little log I'd found was just the right size to carry Cinderella to the ball. Mother could not appreciate my imagination. She was aghast! But I had no one to play with, until one sunny June day some little boy came to play with me. Although he spoke Hungarian and I didn't, there was no communication problem. At first we went to pick wildflowers, buttercups, daisies, bachelor buttons, and poppies. Then we collected June bugs. They were bigger than those I have since seen in the United States. We piled them up in an arena we made of sand. A few would fly away, but most of them stayed, crawling all over each other. Then the little boy had a bright idea, which I followed immediately. We took a flower, broke off the stem really short and inserted the flower in the soft part of the June bug's body. We threw it up in the air and it flew away. Hurriedly, we did the same to the next one and then to the next. It was so much fun to watch the flowers fly away. Our little sky was full of them, and we were in ecstasy. You had to admit it was a happy sight! We started clapping our hands and laughing so loud that it attracted the boy's parents, thus ending our game. Adults always come along and spoil a child's game!

At the bottom of the many steps, leading from the castle, was a barn for Milje the cow and a shed for a few chickens acquired by trading milk, cream, and butter. Milk was our trading currency. Mister Fox quickly found the chickens. At first he only came at night for one, then another night for another (there were no materials or tools to make the shed fox-proof). Then one night he decided to kill all of them. Some he carried off and some he left. Our egg supply was gone! Poor mother, she had to survive blow after blow, defeat after defeat.

Spring was garden-planting time. We had a few beans and a few potatoes. Mother would dig the holes, and I would put in a whole potato, cover it by hand with earth and then stomp on the hole with my foot. We did not know that we could have quartered the potatoes, making sure that there was at least one or more eyes on each piece, which would be enough to sprout and grow a new potato. This would have provided a more abundant crop, allowing us to still save some potatoes to eat.

Poverty and hunger were rampant in all of central Europe during the 1920's. This was a result of the widespread devastation of crops and fields during World War I. Trenches were often dug as the battles were fought. As the tanks and infantry moved on, the fields were ruined, abandoned and left to waste. Below the castle, the entire village was suffering. We all shared the same fate. It took years to replenish the crops. Too often, people had to eat most of the seeds reserved for planting. Harvests were meager.

Once every two to four weeks, mother would bake bread with flour bought with our milk currency. This was a day-long event. The bread was kneaded by hand in a wooden trough about three feet long with fresh sour dough yeast prepared a couple of days earlier. A fire had to be kept burning all day in the kitchen stove for constant room temperature warm enough to raise the dough. The wooden trough could hold a lot of dough. The kneading process required a lot of strength. The brick oven was next to the stove. To heat the oven the wood had to be burned inside of it, and then the ashes had to quickly be removed before the round loaves were shoved in. There were many loaves, and the baking had to be accomplished in two sessions. When done, the ashes were still hot enough to bake some potatoes. At times, bread baking was done only once a month, depending on the flour we could receive from bartering. What a yummy treat the freshly baked bread was! Whole wheat bread would keep a long time in a cool pantry, so we could enjoy our bread for quite some time. The pantry was also where we kept root vegetables: carrots, onions, potatoes, buried in the sand—a very good preservative—away from rats and creeping things.

One day, as the bread dough was raising in a trough on the kitchen table, I had the not-so-bright idea of seasoning it with sand. I mixed sand into it, mixed and kneaded, and mixed some more while mother was busy at her art work. I was still busy when she came back. With horror she stared at what I had done. Today, I can understand her anger at me and her dismay over the loss of the bread and her hard labor. After all, it had meant milking the cow at daybreak, carrying the milk from house to house, trying to exchange it for some flour, slowly amassing enough flour to bake a few loaves for ourselves and maybe even to barter with. In a moment it was gone. I can see her trying to salvage some of the dough and maybe she did. I was oblivious to the consequences but I did realize that I was about to receive the thrashing of my life, and I was not about to be caught. I ran around the table two or three times, got my thrashing anyway, and went to bed deflated. No supper that night! Oh, how painful it was—not the thrashing so much as not getting to eat some fresh hot buns out of the oven.

I was about seven when Mother announced that I simply had to learn to read and write. That was indeed an unexpected announcement, and I asked, "What for? Why?" I was perfectly content and kept myself very busy. In good weather I was with Milje in the pastures, playing in the woods and eating my fill of berries, wild strawberries, blackberries, and some kind of wild raspberries, and in the fall I found hazelnuts. In general, I was always able to find something to eat, even if only sour grass, leaves, and tree bark. Milje and I would come home at sunset, satisfied and not at all hungry. Mother was not concerned for me during the day, for Milje treated me like her calf, and she would surely bring me home. There were times when I would become entangled in a bush or a tree. Then I simply called, "Milje, come Milje!" and she would come close enough to hold onto her horns, climb over her face to her neck and to safety. Occasionally she would lead me to a brook, and we both would drink to our thirst's delight. What a babysitter! What a nanny!

Now in the evenings, I was to learn to read and write. We found out that I was left-handed, and writing left-handed was not acceptable in those years in Europe. I had a terrible time holding a pencil with my right hand, so I had to hide from mother or wait for her to leave the room. When alone, I quickly changed hands and finished my homework. Looking at it, mother would ask, "Did you write this with your left hand?"

"No" I would quickly answer.

Then, "With your right hand?"

"Yes!" I assured her.

"You are lying!" She firmly stated.

"How do you know?" I queried.

"Your eyes turn green when you lie."

I dared not to lie to anyone after that! What I did not know was that my eyes were green anyway, but the writing gave me away immediately. It was from right to left and the letters were reversed. It made no difference to me. I could not see what the fuss was all about. To my young eyes it was all the same. Whether you turned a letter one way or the other it was still the same letter. Even today, I can still read reverse writing.

An astonishing event happened to our small family: Milje gave birth to a calf. I was in awe. Shortly after this, grandmother came to visit us from Vienna, and she commented on my big tummy (a sign of malnourishment). Having recently seen Milje deliver a calf, it was no surprise when I answered proudly and with confidence, "Oh!" putting my hand on my tummy, "I'm going to have a baby!" Can't you just see everyone freezing, eyes bulging, everyone horrified? My grandmother was as strait-laced and Victorian as you could possibly imagine. The adults' horror was not so much at what I had said as at the fact that I said it in front of grandmother. They knew I did not know what I was talking about, so it all promptly dissipated.

Up until then, I had been a happy, resourceful child. I did not know that I was poor, very poor, with not much more than the clothes on my back. I was an only child and seldom had playmates. There were no toys, no candy, no birthday parties, or holidays; however, I didn't realize my poverty and kept very busy and happy, always singing. There was always something to explore, and I enjoyed being with animals, both big and small.

Dear Mother!

Mother went through so much during her short life span. She had married in 1913. The wedding was a sensation as the couple drove through town in an elegant open carriage drawn by a new breed of palomino-like horses harnessed in white chamois. This was a marriage of love. The whole town had turned out to watch the procession. After that she went to Darmstadt, Germany, where father was studying engineering. Mother often helped with his homework at the drafting table. As the professor returned a drawing of a steam-powered locomotive, he told my father, "Judging by the size of the throttle, do you intend to have a woman drive this locomotive?" This speaks well for German precision. Father was embarrassed. Indeed mother had drawn the throttle according to the size of her own hand.

In the summer of 1914, while they were still in Darmstadt, a German official came to their apartment to warn them of the international trouble brewing on the horizon and suggested it would be best for them to leave the country so as not to be imprisoned, being Russian citizens. They followed the advice and went to visit the Pyramids in Egypt, just at the time the Archduke Franz Ferdinand was assassinated in Sarajevo, triggering off the First World War. Father did not get called into the army until 1915, and then he was sent to the Balkans, where the action came later.

I was born that November of 1915. Father came for a visit or two, but I remember nothing about him because he simply stopped coming home. He divorced mother while she was still in Russia. This was more devastating to her than the war. One just did not divorce in those days, and she felt so ashamed.

By 1916 the wounded were being brought in by the hundreds, and mother, in a nurse's uniform, joined many other Russian women to care for men of all nationalities—friends and enemies alike. Mother worked in Odessa first, and later in Sebastopol. Sebastopol was graced by Florence Nightingale during the Balkan war.

In 1918 the war ended, but the revolution had only begun, and by the end of it, a life-long battle for survival began for my mother. She had no nationality and no right to work. The League of Nations in Geneva issued a Nansen passport to be used as identification papers for those Russian refugees who had declined the new USSR passport. These courageous ones were not about to become citizens of a Communist country, so they became citizens without a country, and without the right to hold a legitimate job. Work was scarce even for the self-employed, for after the famine came the depression. For many it was a hand-to-mouth existence, and mother was just one of the many.

When I reflect upon my mother I can see how brave and resourceful she was, full of common sense. I, on the other hand, was reckless, careless, and unappreciative. Because I was alone, having no playmates, I grew totally self-centered, ignorant of others around me, including my mother. I lived in my own little world. I ignored adults, maybe because they, being too preoccupied with poverty, ignored me, but mother cared for me the best she could.

If only we had listened, we would not have been in this dilemma, a result of the total loss of the family fortune.

Mother was brought up in a house full of servants as a refined aristocrat with a French governess and a tutor. An Italian painter taught her the art of drawing and painting, which won her the first prize for portraiture in all of Russia at the age of sixteen. At the age of eighteen, she was also introduced to the court of the Czar. Russian, French, German and English were spoken by all members of her family and of my father's family.

Academic education was of little avail when we were simply trying to survive, yet in the midst of scarcity and constant adversity, she persevered without money, living by her wits. She learned to wash, scrub, and cook, to milk and feed the cow, and to clean the barn. She learned to barter with Hungarian peasants, not even knowing their language. She planted a vegetable garden, baked bread, sawed wood for the stove, made baskets out of willow branches, rope out of flax, and managed to buy some fine wooden boxes which she decorated in Russian folk art using wood burning tools and wood dyes. These colorful and pretty boxes were striking in beauty against the bleak and dull grays of our life and the castle where we lived. I was so impressed by them! Such beauty flowed out of my mother that it surprised me. An overseer of the Weiss family would visit from Budapest occasionally bringing unfinished boxes, tools, and dyes. He would come back several weeks later to pick up the work and sell it. Mother would also give him some jewelry to sell. Obviously, he was able to sell some of the items because he returned with a couple of small horses black as ravens and no more than five feet tall. They came complete with harnesses and a cart to fit. They were mean, biting creatures, and mother had to muzzle them with muzzles she made like baskets, out of willow branches. Evidently they had been mistreated. Although I had to keep my distance, I was allowed to drive them after one short lesson given by my mother.

We had no books, but mother knew many children's stories and fairy tales, poems and songs. Those were happy moments in winter when she had more time and the heart to entertain me. I loved to hear the stories over and over again, and Cinderella was my favorite. I could relate to the poor little girl, and at bedtime when I prayed with my mother, I asked for blessing not only for my family, not only for food, but always for blankets for the poor. I had a soft heart for them without being aware that we were really poor ourselves. I do not recall mother ever complaining nor making me aware of our dire situation; therefore, not knowing any better, I did not expect anything, I did not want.

3

The Orphanage

Where is Milje?

Suddenly, and in a matter of hours, my childhood seemingly collapsed. First it was the cow. I went to the barn to look for mother and I found her attending to the horses, but neither Milje nor the calf were there: "Mama, where is Milje?"

"I sold her. She's gone."

"Gone! No! No! No!"

I burst into a torrent of tears. "No!" It just can't be! How can you sell something that is part of the family? "Come back, Milje, come back!"

I was totally beside myself. I was jumping, running in circles, beating at my mother with my fists. My hurt was uncontrollable. She came and tried to wash my face with cold water to calm me down, to tell me that she had to sell her in order to buy food for me to bring to school. That made it even worse.

"What? Why? I don't want to go to school!" But the decision had been made. That's the way it was to be. There was nothing for me to do but go back to bed at mid-morning and cry myself to sleep.

I could not face it. I slept until the following morning. Mother had already gone out. I found her by the barn with the horses. In the cart there were, maybe, six burlap bags of grains and potatoes. The weather matched my mood; it was gray, cold, and drizzly.

"We will go for a nice long ride" said mother, trying to comfort me. I had nothing to say. I was silenced, dumbfounded, beaten to the ground. I didn't even want to drive the horses. It was to be the gloomiest ride of my young life. How terrible it must have also been for mother; how much she must have suffered. She hadn't told anyone, but she had no choice but to move into town in order to find work and place me in an orphanage. Only she knew that it was to an orphanage that we were headed that day.

After what seemed like an endless buggy ride, we came to a very high, old stone wall with a dilapidated wooden double door. It was centuries old. Mother pulled the cord to ring the bell and a strangely-dressed person in black came out wearing white wings on her head. It scared me. Some words and sign language were exchanged by them. The doors swung open, and we drove into the inner court. Another such person with wings came to lead me away. My heart sank into my heels; my insides froze. I could not recall anything. I do not remember when mother left, nor what I did the rest of the day. I was paralyzed. When I slowly came out of my shock, it was to another world. It seemed like a dungeon, but it was actually a convent—with black and white winged creatures. They were nuns of Saint Vincent, and they seemed to be talking to me, but to no avail. I did not understand. I was given a piece of black bread with lard. Then it was bedtime, and I was shown to a dark corner with a pile of straw. A couple of little girls were sleeping in the straw already. I laid down feeling like a beaten dog, overwhelmed by the experiences of that day. I fell into a deep sleep. The next morning, to my shame, I had wet my "bed." The straw was easy to carry away to the manure pile, but what about my clothes? Well, something had to be done about them and it didn't matter what, but from that night on and during the next three years of orphanage life, I wet every night, to my shame and dismay. It happened almost always while I dreamt beautiful dreams. Of course, the only time I could relax was in my dreams. My heart relaxed, and so did my bladder. This was my first and worst experience there.

The next hard experience I had was with the language — Hungarian. I do not think that I knew more than ten words. The Hungarian language is an Asiatic language dating back to the invasion of the Huns, who remained there because of the rich grasses—the steppes, which grew so tall that they swallowed a man on horseback and were fodder for the horses.

The third worst experience I had was learning to write with my right hand. Mother had already tried to teach me unsuccessfully. Now there was no way out of it. Every time I picked up my pen with my left hand, a dark creature was right there holding a ruler, which would come down on my fingers mercilessly, day after day, until I no longer held the pen with my left hand and had learned to distinguish right from left. Actually, I still have a problem. I still have a repressed desire to write from right to left. By the end of the year I did learn to write and to speak the language with the ability of an eight-year-old. Mother received and kept my report card for years with pride. The marks were very good and some, even excellent.

I only remember two pleasant things about the whole year. The first was the nightly dish of baked potato with a lot of well-fried onions. I looked forward to my supper, which gave me comfort. The other was the birth of a baby goat. I was allowed to play with it from time to time, and it brought relief from my dreary life, so much so that I wrote about it to mother, who had to go to the Hungarian embassy in Vienna and have my letter translated at top translator's prices, only to find out about the baby goat! Poor Mother! This was at a time when she still had very little money.

I do not remember what we did to keep clean. It certainly wasn't much because, shortly after my arrival my head started itching. I was handed a short little object and told to comb my hair with it. It was a fine-toothed comb. My hair was long and very thick. In those days cutting a girl's hair was unheard of. I could not handle such operations, and the dark creature helped me. To start out she dipped the comb into smelly kerosene, combed it through a small clump of hair, and showed me a kind of bug. It was a louse, and my head was full of them! No wonder I and the other girls had started itching all over. This delousing operation was repeated every Saturday with very little success. Although we brushed our hair, there were no toothbrushes to brush our teeth.

Sunday was chapel day. My only recollection is of a dim, eerie, and gloomy place, which I did not like. A certain nun, thinking she was doing me a favor, asked me to change the water of the altar flowers. One whiff of the decayed and petrified stems did it. That was the end of that. No coaxing would help. I just wouldn't do it. This was one of the few times I asserted myself and triumphed. (Some One bigger was on my side.)

At the orphanage the nuns checked at the front door every morning to see if any villagers had left some milk or vegetables or other foods for the orphans. Mother had left me there because I had a better chance of surviving. Milje had paid part of my way to the orphanage. The heavenly Father continued watching over me. He fed me as a sparrow.

Lord, what were you teaching me during those smileless and loveless years? I lived through them for the most part, in a state of numbness. However, I never despaired. I expected and demanded nothing, yet time and again a piece of blue sky or a ray of sunshine brought happiness to my lonely heart. I surely learned to be satisfied with what came my way, without complaining. How precious these lessons have been throughout my life. They have been woven into my character. I learned to share what little I had and instinctively knew not to borrow. I do not borrow even today. I refuse to carry credit cards. To live on borrowed time and money is a disgrace. It is trespassing against the divine principle: "Owe no man anything." Not owing any man has been my life-long principle.

4

Years of Survival: Austria

Life is God's university. Nothing is left to chance; all is planned with a divine purpose. Who would have dreamed that God was preparing a vessel for Himself in this little miserable-looking girl. Experience by experience, something of eternal value was being wrought into me. "The mills of God grind slowly, but they grind exceeding small."

At the end of my first school year in the summer of 1924, someone picked me up at the orphanage in Hungary and brought me to Vienna, Austria, to my mama. My grandmother and my Aunt Olga were also there. I must have been too bewildered to remember anything except that I received a new dress! It was hand-crocheted of crocodile green wool yarn. I wore it for two years. As I grew, it stretched. Being cleaned up and dressed up still did not improve my appearance. I walked pigeon-toed and had a big pear-shaped belly. My sinuses were completely stuffed up and I could only breathe through my mouth. It was hard to eat and breathe at the same time. I could not eat with my mouth closed. Something had to be done quickly

Mother brought me to a children's hospital, a cheerful, light place surrounded by green gardens. Smiling people welcomed me, but again I could not understand them. I did remember some Russian when speaking with Mother and Grandmother, but my Hungarian, which I had learned so painstakingly, did not help me now. As before, sign language of my own design became a handy international form of communication. After seeing the doctor, I was led to a schoolroom on a terrace by the gardens. Everything looked cheerful. I was given books, pencils, color crayons and paper. I felt cared for, which made me feel very good, and I responded gratefully. The eating area was on the top floor next to the sleeping quarters. But while the eating place was enclosed and had large open windows, the sleeping quarters had only a partial roof, like a carport over a long row of beds. We slept in the wide open spaces for the sake of our health and played on the roof terrace. There was an enclosed gym for rainy days. Plenty of fresh air was a form of rehabilitation, which I desperately needed after the musty and smelly orphanage.

Except for one incident, I was happy at the hospital. All was bright and white and clean. On one occasion, as I was eating my dinner, an extra plate was brought in covered with some white pieces of food that smelled horrible. It reminded me of the decaying flowers on the altar. I was forced to eat it. I couldn't. Everyone had already gone to play. I was left alone at the table. Little by little, I swallowed the food, holding my nose, and at the end, it came right up onto the plate. I was crying hard. Well, that was not the end of the story. Another plateful came along, and the same ordeal was repeated three times. I was told the cauliflower was very good for me and very healthful. On the third time around, however, something wonderful happened, suddenly the cauliflower tasted good, very good, and I have liked it ever since. Some One came to my rescue. Some One compassionate was watching over me.

I loved to prance around the garden. Time and again an adult would call me in an angry voice, this time in German, "Helene!" In Hungary, it was "Ilonka!" In Russian, it was "Yelena!" People were angry at me, that much I could tell. But most of the time, I did not know what they were angry about as

I could not understand their language. Later on, in France, *they* called to me, "Hélène!" and jeered something to me, which I still could not understand. All of this shouting and name-calling caused a negative reaction in me. "What had I done now?" I asked myself out of a sense of fear, but not out of guilt. For years following, when hearing my name called, my inner response was fear, "What have I done now?"

At the start of the next school year, I was taken from the hospital and brought miles out of Vienna to a very large two-story castle with four towers, one at each corner. The roof was black; the walls, a light cream color. There was a good sized inner court with shrubs. This is good so far, I thought. My heart sank however, when once again, winged creatures received me. I was petrified. As usual, I didn't understand the language (German); however, the atmosphere was brighter than the orphanage in Hungary. In this convent-school, many smiling girls were playing and running. The day of my arrival was still vacation time; school was to start the following morning. Classes were to be taught in German, of course.

Meanwhile, I became acquainted with our toilet facilities, real toilets, with running water from a tank two meters over my head, and with a long chain which I pulled to release the water, just like the ones in Vienna. There was a row of washbowls to wash our hands and face in the morning, and occasionally our arms and feet. There were still no toothbrushes, no baths, and no showers. But, there was a little fine toothed comb and yes, the lice would return.

The dormitory was a spacious room with lots of windows and two rows of beds. There probably were a dozen beds to a row. Mine was to be the fourth. The mattress was filled with straw because of my bed-wetting, but at least, it was a mattress! In all, my new home was a big improvement over the Hungarian orphanage. The most striking thing to me was the parquet hardwood floor. After chapel time, our first job in the morning was to get the steel wool, the wax, and the brush, in order to shine these floors until they were glistening. After learning to do it, I made a game of it and had fun. Such exercise helped dispel my morning shame and guilt for wetting the bed. A few other girls my age, who were nine years old, had the same problem and received the same reprimand day after day. These were crushing blows to one's self-esteem, but by breakfast time something in me would bounce back to face the rest of the day. Although I did not understand the language, it was not as difficult as the year before, for now I knew how to write and to draw. Arithmetic was my favorite subject because at least the numbers didn't change from one language to another.

I also liked the afternoon hours of handiwork. I did not need to speak to learn to sew, crochet, and knit. However, I was startled when given a partially knit stocking out of black thread. Four needles were engaged in the work, and I was to knit new stitches onto a fifth needle. It was a bewildering situation. The nun showed me briefly how to hold the needles and the thread with one finger up in the air. Then she left me on my own. She went down the line to check and help the other girls, leaving me in a dither. By the time she came to me again, I was still working on my first needle. The stitches were uneven, some were twisted, and some had been dropped. I knew it was a mess. The nun was unhappy with me. She did not spank my hands with the ruler this time, but I knew I needed to learn quickly. In my case, it was not necessity, but fear, that was the mother of knowledge.

Thus, I knitted a pair of black stockings for myself. That was a big reward. During these two years at the convent in Judenau by Vienna, I learned to sew, to crochet doilies, to cross-stitch and to knit gloves with all the fingers—not mittens only—but gloves. This ability has stayed with me to my young old age! We had an hour of recreation each day, during which we were free to run and jump and shout. We had some jump ropes and also chalk with which to draw games on the cement of the court. Somersaults were considered indecent exposure and were not allowed. The skirts had to remain below the knee even at play.

Around Christmastime, Mother sent me a toy from Paris, a cloth doll with a big head of curly blonde hair that was very short. We had never seen hair like that. Everyone laughed. The only time I had available to play with her was Sunday afternoon, which was all right with me. I did not know how to play with a doll anyway. Later, I also received a nice bed for her with sheets and a blanket, and I was allowed to sew her dresses.

Life was unfolding in a more human way. Little by little the language barrier was overcome, much of it through singing! Singing! We had never sung in Hungary. I loved to sing even though I was always off-key. We sang lovely songs by Schumann, Schubert, Brahms, and Wagner. Songs such as *Rösslein auf der Heide*, *die Lorelei, Guten Abend Gute Nacht, Stille Nacht Heilige Nacht*, *Edelweiss,* and many others. I did not just sing; I lived them in imagination, just carried away! A few songs were in the Viennese dialect. Do you remember *Mutterl, lieb Mutterl*? In singing, along with gymnastics (I was quite clumsy), my school marks could not rise above what would be the equivalent of a C—all others were A and A+.

When Mother had sent the doll, she also asked that I be given a bath at least once in a while. The once in a while occurred at Christmas and Easter times. I was taken completely apart into a different wing of the building. No one was to see me or even know that I received such privileged treatment. Of course, everyone found out just by looking at me: clean and shining with my hair all wet. The girls would ask, "Why did you receive a bath and not us?"

"Because my mother requested it."

"But we don't have a mother," said one little girl.

That is how I found out that I was in an orphanage again. It didn't affect me as much as the year before when I was engulfed in my own grief, having for all purposes lost my mother. But this time, I really felt sorry for the others. They did not have mothers, when I did. I sensed a surge of love in my heart for the first time. I experienced loving my mother. Although I had hardly seen her in the past year and a half and she was so far away, *still* I had a mother. My frozen insides started to melt. I cried for the girls. The same compassion rose in my heart as when I used to pray for food and blankets for the poor children back in the Hungarian castle. However, our schedule was so busy. There was no time allowed for sentiment and emotion. I suppose this was just as well. We were taught to work, to do what we were told, on time, not to the striking of a clock, but in this case to the sound of a bell in one of the four towers. This was good Austrian discipline and accuracy.

How did we get our food? There were some fields around the convent worked by the nuns. Our potatoes, beets, onions and carrots probably came that way. As for the bread, we received shipments from Vienna consisting of the stale bread collected from the bakeries. And did we get bread to eat! For breakfast there was bread in watered-down milk with a little sugar. For lunch there was bread in the form of soup with a few slices of carrots and fried onions. For supper there was bread with potatoes or noodles. Then there was bread pudding for dessert. Twenty years later, I still gagged at the thought of soaked bread. Well, we were survivors, although my belly got bigger and bigger from a continued lack of protein and my nose stuffier and stuffier. Even a goiter started growing, yet we were alive. We survived, while millions of children were dying of hunger in Russia at that same time.

Mother managed to come and see me once in those two years, and she spent the day delousing me. All I remember of her visit is the smell of kerosene.

In addition to our regular classes, we also had catechism lessons. The teaching seemed unreal to me. The only part that made sense was that there was only one God, that I should obey my parents (in this case the nuns), and that I should not lie or steal. I already knew that. On Saturday we had confession. That was strange. I was required to go into a dark booth and tell my sins to someone sitting in the dark on the other side of a trellis.

What sins? I was not very sin-conscious. I did not lie; I did not steal. So I decided to make up a lie on the spot, and I lied to the *Pfarrer* (priest). That way, I had something to confess the next time.

I did not like chapel time, particularly on winter mornings. It was so cold and dark, and my knees ached so much when kneeling. I tried to arrive there first and sit closer to the candles for warmth. Once in a while I would reach out to warm my hands. However, the worst part of it was probably the chanting of the Gregorian songs, so monotonous, so sad. They gave me the feeling of death. I had experienced that before, during the Revolution. I liked to sing, but you never caught me chanting the Te Deum while playing, as I did with other songs. How could I relate to the chants and apply them to my daily living? They were out of context, and even at that early age I realized religious practices did not touch me. I attended all the church ceremonies as one would a play at the theater. On high holidays they were even more impressive, as shows go.

Before Christmas, we were told to be especially good, and we were given a toy manger each, to be filled little by little with wisps of straw that we would earn by good behavior and good deeds, thus preparing a soft bed for baby Jesus. That manger was supposed to represent our hearts. Becoming very sentimental, I tried hard. On Christmas day we brought our little straw-filled mangers to the village, the scene of a bigger manger, and left them there. It was all very mysterious, but nothing happened, no baby Jesus came, and we forgot all about it.

A few months later we were being prepared for communion. That was to be the best day of our lives. Dressed all in white, we went reverently to the *Pfarrer* at the altar and stuck out our tongues, politely, to receive a little white wafer called a hostie. It was tasteless. But "*hocus, pocus*," it became transubstantiated (I learned this word years later) into the body of Jesus, and by eating it Jesus would come inside of me. A nun said that we would feel something. I had no idea who Jesus was and when asked if I felt differently I said, "No"! I felt disappointment. On that day I was also given a rosary and taught how to use it by saying an *Ave Maria*—yes, in Latin—at every bead. There were fifty of them plus three beads of *Pater Noster.* We all learned to rattle them off at great speed. None of this had anything to do with the sincere prayers of my heart to God when still with mother in Hungary. I pondered this and kept it to myself, because even if I had wanted to, I could not put my feelings into words then.

A little seed of reality, a Treasure, had been planted in my heart and was growing, pushing away anything unreal. Religious practices were unreal things to me. I watched them like you would a show in the theater. Despite my six years in different convents, when it came to religion, I was a silent bystander, only watching. To me religion was a fantasy, outside of the context of life.

5

France

At the end of my second school year in Judenau and at my mother's request, my aunt Olga graciously came for me at the orphanage and brought me to Vienna to prepare me to rejoin my mother in Paris. As a result, I spent a few days in dreamland with real people, not just nuns and with horses! We took a horse-drawn cab (a taxi) to visit friends. The streets of Vienna were running with horse carriages, with an occasional Model T Ford trying to catch up, as cars were still scarce. To me, this was a pretty and a happy sight.

I received so much attention. People actually talked with me, not only at me. One lady asked me why I was walking pigeon-toed. I did not know; no one had said anything about it. She showed me how to walk properly and made me practice. It was no problem. She also told me not to bite off my fingernails, and she trimmed them for me and then made me push back the cuticles with the thumb nail. One nice man folded a bird out of paper for me. By pulling the tail the wings moved. It was flying! I was fascinated and wanted him to teach me how to do it. He wouldn't. "All right then," I said to myself, "I'll do it myself." He softened, seeing I made it half-way through. That little bird has since then thrilled many a poor child I've met through my travels.

On another one of my aunt's visits to some friends, I had a happy experience. We stayed in a villa with a beautiful flower garden, and when I looked out of my bedroom window, there on the lawn was a white rabbit hopping happily along. I jumped for joy. My white rabbit was in front of me on the other side of the window with his soft white fur, red shining eyes, twitching nose, and those talking ears! Running out, I shouted to the adults, "My rabbit! Come and see my rabbit!" He had disappeared! No one could find him, but still, I was happy. Something happened to my heart. The five-year-old wound was healed by my unseen Friend.

The time came to leave Vienna. My next destination was Paris, France, to meet my mother. This time I was going alone and needed identifications. Until now, I had crossed the borders with my mother. Now I needed my own passport. For this I had my picture taken full size in my green crocodile dress, snug around my pearshaped belly, with two thick braids down to my waist. I was perplexed. Now what? Next, the photo was glued to a piece of paper with my name, birthdate, and status: refugee, citizen without a country, just like Mama's. The passport was given with instructions as to what it was for and how to keep it safe. Aunt Olga put it into a small handbag for me to carry all the time until I saw Mother. This was a big charge because I was not accustomed to carrying anything other than my doll, which I dragged along by an arm. I did not care much for her now.

On parting at the station, my aunt's last words were a warning: "You will meet people that do not like Germans. They will talk against them. Do not pay attention. My "Why?" was answered much later. To me, people were all the same—if only they would speak alike. I wondered how they would speak at my next stop. It certainly will be different. "Mama will be surprised at how well I speak German," I thought. As for Russian, I could barely remember it, and there had been no one to speak Hungarian with. It was lost, except for a few greetings and some words: *Jo napot kivannok*, wishing you a good day; *Nem tudom*, I do not know; *Kezi csokolom*, I kiss your hand; *Szep*, pretty; *Igen*, yes, and; *kalapacs*, a hammer. A hammer! Why would a little girl remember such a word? Could it be from the hammering raps with the ruler I received while learning to write?

On the train, the conductor with whom my aunt spoke showed me to a pretty compartment with dark green upholstered seats. A lady sat by the window. I sat by the door, very correctly, my hands in my lap and feet dangling. "Ladies do not cross their legs," was my grandmother's admonition. A long time elapsed. The lady was silent and so was I, still too timid to talk or move. Then she started eating fruit and offered me a banana. "Do you like bananas?" I did not know. This was my first banana. It tasted so good. Later she invited me to come with her to the dinning car. I was so amazed. I cannot recall what I ate.

Back in the cabin I went to sleep. The lady, a friend by now, woke me up. The train had stopped. We were at the French border. Everyone got off. My friend told me I must not forget my handbag with the passport as she escorted me to a couple of unhappy looking men in uniform. They demanded to see my passport in such a rough way. "You are traveling alone? Where is your mother? Where are you going?" They scared me. I could not answer.

My friend talked for me and took me back to our friendly compartment. She was like a guardian angel. Indeed Someone was directing her from behind the scene.

After a long trip of two days and a night the train came to a final stop. "*C'est Paris!*" said my friend. PAREE! shouted the conductor walking down the corridor of the train. We stepped off and I parted with a curtsy. Mother quickly found me in the crowd with my crocodile green dress. The meeting was awkward. We were almost like strangers, having hardly seen one another the past three years. I think we were both embarrassed. No one had hugged me for a long time, and she was not accustomed to it either. She held my hand, and we made our way through a throng of people. The streets were full of carriages and cars. The noise was piercing. Then we took a stairwell to an underground train, a metro. Again, too noisy! I still managed to fall asleep, but not for long. It was time for more steps to the street and then some more to a fourth floor apartment where Mother was taking me to stay with her cousins. I was too exhausted, too hungry, too sleepy to care for the people who lived there. Nothing mattered.

In the morning I realized that these people had known me in Russia, and we had been together during the first months of exile in Constantinople and in Hungary. So much trauma had gone on in between. All but Nadia, my aunt, left for work early in the morning. She worked at home as a dressmaker. She had pretty scraps I could use, and I worked right along beside her, making dresses for my doll. I was trained to be diligent and disciplined. Nadia also cooked for this unusual family of siblings in their forties, my aunt Nadia, with her brothers Georges, and Serge. How enjoyable it was to eat together. Everyone was full of laughter. What a contrast it was with the convents where we were not allowed to talk. It had been too frustrating, and we had all learned the alphabet sign language and talked to our immediate neighbor with our hands hidden under the table! We just had to communicate.

Mother had taken a room with a French woman and worked as a dressmaker for an American family of three girls close to my age. The American woman wanted Mother to come to the United States when they returned. She couldn't bear to leave me behind again and declined their offer. What a pity that she missed the land of opportunity!

The American girls had so many toys, and they invited me to play with them. We had so much fun. They spoke English and French, and I spoke Russian and German. It made us laugh that much more. But at this stage of my life the most enjoyable thing was food. I was finding out that food not only could, but should taste good. We had bananas and cornflakes and cream and sugar. Yummy! To think that the girls ate like this every morning. It was so delicious!

Because of my sinuses, mother took me to a doctor. "All this little girl needs is some good food and minerals. Take this." It was a delicious syrup, probably blackstrap molasses. In that atmosphere of care, food, and play, happy days returned, and I stopped wetting the bed.

Le Midi

Meanwhile, Mother made arrangements with her older brother, Theodore—I called him Uncle Fyedia—to keep me on his farm in southern France for a year. I would start learning French and be relieved from the pressure of convent life. Thank God, "*Slava Bogou!*" Uncle Fyedia also spoke German, and I quickly recalled enough Russian to communicate with the other members of the family, my Aunt Hélène, of Greek origin, and my two cousins Olga and Tatiana. I had been together with this family years before in Constantinople. Aunt Hélène was neither very talkative nor demonstrative, but she cooked us good meals and read us good books in Russian after supper. The books also whetted our appetite for more. Uncle Fyedia came to my rescue, translating into German when I could not understand.

We were tutored at home by a French woman. Mademoiselle, our tutor, was a kind old maid in her seventies, who coached me in French. At first, I was weary of learning another language. She also taught us some rudimentary piano. I did not make it past the second lesson. I didn't seem to have the coordination, much less the ear for music—quite likely affected by my chronic sinus condition. Improper nourishment in my younger years no doubt took its toll.

My cousin Olga was talented in many ways. On Saturdays she had piano lessons in Marseilles. My uncle and aunt went to town at those times in a Model T Ford to take Olga to her lessons and to deliver their farm products to their established customers. Tatiana and I stayed by ourselves. Mademoiselle did not make the trip up the dusty two kilometers on Saturdays. Tatiana and I liked being by ourselves very much when Olga was gone. She gave us so much trouble, bossing us around, making fun of us, hurting us with her air of superiority. True, I had very little prior life experiences having been shut up in orphanages—as in a prison. That gave her plenty of ground. I did not know how to handle this, and I had nightmares about her that lasted for years. I was just now learning to socially relate to people. I do not recall a single friend, girl or nun, from the past three years. Affection had been an unrealized feeling. Yet inwardly I wanted to love. Tatiana was my first friend.

We both liked the rabbits, the chickens, and the pigeons. We had two household pets. One was a white angora rabbit—yes, another rabbit. She came daily to beg for food when let out of her cage. She was not very particular and ate anything from fish to chocolate. We named her Juliette. She was so soft and gentle, at least until she was put in a cage with another rabbit to breed. The only result was a big fight with fur flying. Juliette turned out to be a Romeo.

The other pet was a big plump Wyandott hen, *la Poule*, who would come almost daily cackling and announcing proudly she was about to lay an egg in her peculiar spot in the parlor. We enjoyed their visits for months until one day, we noticed that both pets were missing. Olga, who liked helping her parents dress the chickens and rabbits for the market, had decided to kill *Juliette* and *la Poule* for our dinners. I felt a knife in my stomach. How could she be so heartless? It gives you an idea of her personality. Tatiana and I did not know how to get along with her. We were so different from her.

On my uncle's farm, there were trees to climb, olives to pick, and figs to eat—delicious, tree ripened sun dried figs, which tasted like jam. When grapes were in season, we would go to the vineyard with a chunk of French bread and a piece of cheese to gorge ourselves on a sweet variety of grapes. The Malaga were my favorites. The vineyards were not sprayed and we could eat the grapes right off the branches, warmed by the sun. *O! le soleil du Midi!*

That beautiful sun of southern France was warming me also inwardly. I was emerging from the sad, restrictive, colorless, and stifling existence and developing into a happy little girl. I was so appreciative although, I could not express it. There was a stirring in my heart, a certain drawing I could not understand. It was my Treasure.

On several summer Sundays, I went alone to the Catholic Church in the village a couple of kilometers away. I went searching for *something*. I stood in the back behind a packed throng of people. It did not matter that I could not see, for I had already seen it in Hungary and again in Austria. Only before, it was the *Pfarrer* performing the mass, but now it was the *curé*. The songs were the same Gregorian chants, in Latin, and the same flickering candles trying to break through the darkness. The sound of *mea culpa, mea culpa,* gave me the shivers. Being at the back I could be the first one out, trotting home on a dusty road, often in a scorching sun. Except for having had an outing, I did not feel any more satisfied. I began to sense a void in my heart, a brief, fleeting feeling of an inner, deeper need. The Treasure was stirring.

I can remember feeling so peaceful when on my uncle's farm. If you are acquainted with Cezanne's paintings of southern France, then you will be familiar with the farm, set in rolling hill country, bathed in intense sunlight and deep shadows, the shadows of the Mediterranean pines. These trees yield cones encasing the delicious piñon nuts. Around the base of the trunk grow the Chanterelle mushrooms. What a treat it was to go mushroom hunting with the family after a good rain. Closer to the house were laurel bushes, olive groves, almond trees, and best of all, the vineyard.

The house was a primitive white-washed structure with a red tile roof. The front door, which was most always open, was flanked by a window on either side. The second floor also had two windows, one for each bedroom. There was nothing symmetrical about the structure. The front door was also the window to the main room of the house. The furniture in that room consisted of a round table with a number of chairs around which centered most of the activities of the day: the three meals, the tutoring, the homework, the hand sewing, the nightly reading, and the packing of farm products for the weekly trip to the market. The kitchen, on the right, with one of the windows, was my aunt's domain. The left window opened to the parlor where the piano stood. The parlor was Olga's domain. In it was also a chest of drawers with Uncle's memorabilia from Russia. One time only, he showed us the elegant uniform he wore as a member of the Czarina's private mounted guard. His plumed brass helmet remained in Russia. It was too cumbersome to be brought out. We had only seen it in photos. He was very dashing then on his beautiful horse. No one lingered much on the past. As a result, I knew so little about it.

The bedrooms were quite roomy, and ours served as a playroom as well. However, it was intended for use by the human kids and not for the goat's kid. We had managed to sneak a baby goat upstairs one evening, where it slept in one or another of the beds all night. The problem only flourished in the morning when we all started to jump around and have a pillow fight. The goat promptly gored the pillow case, and feathers flew all around, to our delight. All of this commotion attracted Uncle Fyedia and we ended up with a generous paddling. It was worthwhile, however, for I remember the fun, and not the paddling.

Two other buildings close to the house were a barn and a *pigeonier* with pigeon holes. Pigeons were in abundance. We ate them if Olga could keep track of their hatching. You must catch them while still in their nest and exactly thirty days old, the day before they fly the coop. They were delicious, finer than chicken.

The spring of 1927 was quite an eventful time. All in our village were so excited because a man had flown over the Atlantic in a plane. Everyone was talking about Charles Lindbergh. His plane, *The Spirit of St. Louis,* had landed at the Bourget Field near Paris. It took some explaining for me to comprehend it, but we all enjoyed the village celebration and the dancing to the music of accordions. I had never seen anything like it. This was fun. You could kick up your heels in rhythm, and I did! The Charleston had made its debut in the village, having come a thousand kilometers from Paris, and to Paris all the way from across the Atlantic.

Soon, the school year would be coming to an end and so were my happy days at the farm.

6

Belgium

After much searching for and inquiring about a boarding school, mother met an abbot at his office in Paris who, as far as I can tell, must have been in charge of the schools in different convents. She pleaded with him to take me in and forego the tuition. He was an understanding man. He knew about the plight of the Russian refugees and their poor civil status, and came to Mother's assistance in a generous way. I was placed in an elite convent for the education of the girls of French nobility. That part did not mean a thing to me; I was not impressed. What I did relate to was a smiling nun all dressed in white. She welcomed me at the station and carried my small bag containing two uniforms made by Mother, two pairs of hose, one black and one white pair for Sunday, and underwear.

We walked a short distance to an impressive iron gate. We entered into an open garden through a side door, and there it was, a beautiful Tuilleries-like building like the one in Paris, only smaller. It had been built during the French Revolution when the nuns were persecuted and went either into hiding or into exile. And so, it remained a French convent and boarding school. All the nuns were French, and so were the furnishings and the food. This time I was not in shock.

The nuns wore white according to the order of Saint Bernardine and I was treated like a real person. The dormitory was partitioned into private bedrooms. A nun led me to my private quarters, and she helped me put my things in order. I had my own chest of drawers with an earthenware washbowl, water pitcher, and a wardrobe. She asked me to wash up and put on my uniform with the black stockings. One time, when I could not find both of my black stockings in the morning rush, I simply put a white one on the other foot. To me a stocking was a stocking, the color made no difference. I wasn't a bit style-conscious at twelve. I was just happy to have something to wear. The nice nun told me that this did not look pretty, and she found the other one under the bed. I had to learn to keep my things in order now that I had more than one choice. I learned to be neat and clean. We even had a bath every Saturday!

There were no more than twenty girls of all ages, with two to three to a classroom with different tutors. It was wonderful. I needed that attention, but when it came to Latin and Greek, I rebelled. No more languages, please! Some One understood and prevailed. I was excused from Latin and Greek.

The dining room was a cheerful place with French windows which opened to a garden. It had several tables with six chairs each. We sat by age groups and were allowed to talk to but not to fraternize with the senior students. I soon developed a loving admiration for a particular senior girl. She was so beautiful, so near and yet so far away. She did not respond to my longing to hug her and be her friend. I suffered. My loving admiration was crushed.

In the recreation hall the girls my age took advantage of my poor French and taught me some songs in secret. I did not understand what kind of songs they were and so I sang them wholeheartedly, out of tune, to the nuns. I even stood up on the table giving a performance, dancing the Charleston. The songs turned out to be street songs. *Elle avait des tous petits petons, Valentine, Valenton!*....etc. Those who have heard the rest can imagine the horror on the nuns' faces. I was oblivious to it, and innocent. Could they not understand that?

Later, I wondered where an aptitude for performing had come from. It must have come from Vienna when I had gone to recuperate and Mother took me to the Opera to introduce me to some culture. At the price of deprivation, we went to see *Hansel und Gretel*, ballet and all. Although I slept through most of it, an impression remained stored in my subconscious. Grandmother Schwachheim reminded me that after the Opera I performed for her using a white garden table as my stage. No one can tell me that children are not formed by their environment.

My experience of a few years before had surfaced at the worst possible time and place. To add insult to the adults' injury, I innocently asked the nuns what they did with their babies. Where were the babies? Every woman was supposed to have a baby! My life had been that sheltered! Obviously, no one believed I could be so naive. There was no response from the nuns. Two years later, I asked Mother for an explanation of childbirth and told her of my behavior in Mons, Belgium. "No wonder," said Mother. "This explains it all. I received a letter dismissing you from the convent for not being proper material to be a nun." She sobbed because she had had to look yet again for another school and I had to go through much more adjustment. How poor the educators were in those days! All I needed was a simple explanation and guidance. Yet my invisible Guide allowed it for His purpose. I was not destined for the nunnery. He was molding me for another goal.

When I left the convent in Belgium at the end of the school year, to rejoin Mother in Paris, there was no one to pick me up at the station. The father of a schoolmate waited with me a while and then asked me if I would like to go home with them. I gladly accepted and had a fun experience. They lived in Versailles in a cozy home at walking distance to *Le Palais de Versailles*. We went to play there, either in the palace or on the formal grounds. I noticed that there were no bathrooms in the palace. I assumed that in those glamorous days you simply had to hide behind a door to relieve yourself into chamber pots!

When asked for names and addresses of my mother and my relatives, I did not know any more than their first names. My mother, Hélène, had resumed her maiden name. Then, there were Aunt Nadia and Uncle Georges. Where did he work? After thinking hard I came up with *Pétrole,* from a conversation I had overheard, some company to do with petroleum. My kind host went down every company name in the phone directory related to the subject and asked everywhere for Georges. On the third day, he found him at the *Consommateur de Pétrole*. Coming home after work, my host announced with a sigh of relief that my aunt Nadia, who had been late in coming to the station, would now pick me up. Every one was relieved except for my playmate and me. She was an only child. Her mother had passed away and we had had a very good time for three whole days.

Scouts on the French Riviera

A big surprise was awaiting me. Mama was searching for some place for me to be occupied in the summer. She contacted the Russian nobility (not all were penniless). There must have been one hundred thousand Russian refugees in Paris, and they were quite well organized in numerous clubs: social clubs, art clubs, schools, sports for all ages, banquets, etc. Among them were ex-statesmen, governors and mayors, generals and admirals, and notorious noblemen. One of them had established Russian Boy Scout and Girl Scout clubs. I was enrolled. We were given khaki uniforms and a Scout hat like the boys. I was flabbergasted and did not know what to think of it. We had a meeting, about twenty of us, and were told that we were going camping to the Riviera for the two summer months. This was certainly something new and different, but I had no problem adjusting. This was fun, yet I learned so much. We set up camp, four girls to a tent. Everything had to be just so. When the camp was awakened every morning, we stood at attention, sang a prayer in Russian, and saluted the French flag in French, all before breakfast. For a couple of hours afterward, we had a variety of activities to learn all about scouting, its goal, purposes, and history. Baden Powell, the founder of scouting, was our ready-made hero and we worked hard to earn badges.

There was a lot of time to play and swim in the afternoon. The camp was set up on the isle of St. Marguerite facing Cannes in the beautiful Mediterranean Sea. The camp sat on the square in front of the ruins of an old fort. Legend had it that Napoleon's illegitimate son was brought up and educated there in seclusion. This set our imaginations soaring. Three of us joined to form the Three Musketeers—Atos, Portos, Aramis—to come to His Majesty's rescue. Historical chronology did not concern us a bit. In the dark hours of the evening we would storm the fort, invade the different roofless rooms, and scare one another to death. Fright would bring our daring to an end. This game went on evening after evening until we overcame fright and lost interest. To this day I am not afraid of the night.

Then, it was time to sleep, that is, if you could ward off the mosquitoes. They were fierce! You had to cope with them for three weeks, after which time you developed an immunity and slept like a log.

Most of the afternoons were spent in the water away from the heat. I did not know how to swim and decided to learn fast. St. Marguerite is a big rock, with no sandy beaches. The girls would jump off a pier. I watched them carefully go under and come up. That seemed simple enough. They came up every time and so would I. I spotted the big pillars about four meters apart, holding up the pier. I decided to jump close to one and hold onto it. I came up, held on, and paddled dog fashion to the next, heading for the shore. It worked so well that I gained confidence and decided to give some style to my swimming. The waters of the Mediterranean Sea, being very salty, are also very buoyant. Just to learn the breast stroke, however, took me the rest of the summer. I was very clumsy and uncoordinated and it took some effort.

We also had K.P. duty, and I learned to cook for two dozen people. I loved it. My cooking was liked even though everybody vomited after eating my delicious pear compote. I had cooked the pears in an aluminum pan and let them sit a couple of hours, enough time for the acidity of the pear to react with the metal. No more aluminum pans for me.

We were chaperoned by two of the girls' mothers and our eighteen-year-old capable Scoutmaster. She was very beautiful. These Girl Scout summer camps were such a relief from the drudgery of convent life. The Great Physician was silently healing me, strengthening me inwardly and outwardly through pleasant circumstances. I was relating to the other girls and particularly to some of their mothers. Even at the end of the first summer I was prepared to face another year at another convent.

Colombier: Another Convent

This time, I was not sent far away. The convent in Colombier was only an hour away by street car from Paris. Surely mother would come to visit me. She seldom came. One Sunday afternoon my heart was crying out for my mother; the visiting hours were half over. She did not come, and I simply walked out of the gate and followed the tram tracks, trying to make all the necessary turns at the crossroads. I must have walked for three hours. Night was closing in when I rang the door bell. The door opened and there was my mother...Mama! I was in tears from an overpowering emotion and fatigue. Mother was so stunned as I embraced her. She had been renting a room, so my unexpected coming created a problem as to what to do with me. The landlady's words were harsh, something to the effect that it was much too late to send me back to the convent and that I could spend the night with Mother, but only for this time. Her words had no effect on me, they did not penetrate. "*Sufficient unto the day is the evil thereof.*" I had had enough.

Toward the end of the second year, I could take convent life no longer. The nuns in black were like moving statues to me. I was tired of lentil soup twice a day, tired of sleeping in a big dorm with countless others, tired of eating in a cafeteria with two long tables and benches just as long. I was tired of the gray and sterile atmosphere and liturgy, tired of all the impersonal treatments. There was no friendship, no love, only the law and corrections. It was in exact opposition to our Girl Scout training with its code of honor and care, developing in us a sense of propriety and dignity.

Again I have no recollection of any particular nun, and I had only two friends. We would meet in the bathroom on Saturdays, the day for foot-washing. Twelve basins of water were set up and girls came twelve at a time. Three of us were exempt. We received special treatment and did not participate in the foot-washing activities. Our mothers insisted with the Mother Superior that we be given a weekly bath instead. The two other girls were daughters of a Spanish attaché at their embassy in Paris, and were accustomed to a better life in Madrid. This bathing session turned out to be riotous. There were two tin bathtubs with a heavy sheet hanging from two circles from the ceiling, and enveloping the tubs. We had to get our head through the circle and undress and wash under the sheet. Since nakedness was sinful, we should not even see our own selves. By that time we were already hysterical and carried on and on. Should we soap ourselves under the sheet or over it? The poor nun was exasperated. She punished us the following Saturday with foot-washing. It was no solution, because we made the others laugh to the point of being hysterical; therefore we went back to the baths. It was a most enjoyable time, the only fun I remember.

By the end of the second year in Colombier, something within me rose up and I made a daring and spontaneous declaration to Mother, "You put me back there and I'll run away, and you will never find me." I was shocked at my own words. This was not a way to talk to any adult. I expected a slap or something but Mother never said a word and I was not sent back to the convent. I cried out and Someone delivered me.

Today I can see and appreciate a little of my Teacher's plan. During those six years of convent life I was sheltered from much evil. I was fed during famines, disciplined, and taught to be diligent. Because of my proud heritage, I needed much breaking of self and shaping of character, or I might have turned into a modern Ivan the Terrible, female edition. I had to be put into the crucible of life at an early age.

7

The World Spread Before Me

More Schooling, More Scouting

The Paris school administration did not esteem convent education very highly and made me repeat my last year of junior high. Ironically, I was actually ahead of the public school, which made my studies easy, and I had plenty of time to catch up with reading. At the convent, apart from a very restricted list of classical literature like Racine, Molière, Corneille, La Fontaine, plus excerpts from Victor Hugo, Dumas, Boileau, etc., we had no choice and no access to books. However, of those mentioned we could recite pages at a time. That was excellent training in language, composition, grammar, and style. It did give us a good, solid background. The public schools' reading requirement was more extensive. The library was wide open to the pupils, and I took advantage of it. I did like classic historical novels, but what enthralled me were books on nature and detective stories. Jack London, Ellery Queen, and Sherlock Holmes were my favorites, translated into French, of course.

Outwardly, my first year away from the convent seemed a loss of time as learning goes. Homework was a breeze. I was at the head of the class and had no problems, but the Wise Planner gave me this time to adjust to real life outside of a convent. There was so much to learn about everyday living and responsibilities at home. Mother was at work all day. I could help with some shopping and even cooking, but I was very awkward at everything, truly an ugly duckling. Mother and I had moved into a small attic room—we shared the bed. I was willing to sleep on the floor at the head of the stairs. Anything was better than the convent. We had a little table by a small window on the stair landing where we ate and cooked on one kerosene burner. One day something happened, and I talked back to mother. A slap came flying my way, landing right on my left cheek. Although I was already fifteen, children were not allowed to talk back to their parents. I needed a reminder. That was the last. Nothing eventful happened that year, and I could look forward to another Girl Scout camp on the Riviera.

This time we camped near Antibes, another enchanted spot on the bluest sea. During that time the Scoutmasters laid out a march route for the girls. We started our march from the French-Italian border town of Menton. We were to reach a village in the hills of the back country. A dozen of us started out with our pretty Scoutmaster. One of the girls had a bugle. She played that bugle very well, and we enjoyed the numerous echoes. After a few hours of intensive hiking, we were stopped by two armed mountain police. The echoes of the bugle had alerted the French border patrol. They interpreted them as signals to the Italian *carabinieri* and led us to a nearby army camp, to be interrogated. Our chieftain spoke for us and cleared the air. We were thought of as being spies. Unbeknownst to us, we were following the Italian border giving signals with the bugle! All was quickly settled. The army was at ease and invited us for lunch. Furthermore, the officer in charge provided us with an escort to our destination that we needed to reach by supper time. No more bugle, but we could sing, and sing we did.

As we arrived at the village, we were drenched to the core because of a rainstorm. Our guide asked us to wait a moment at the village fountain. Upon his return, he gave us the good news that we could come out of the rain and take refuge at the police station. Why not! "Always prepared!" was our slogan, and we were always ready for adventure. Except for the two policemen, the place was empty. We could see the jail cells with empty bunks. We were reassured not to be afraid. We could trust them and even spend the night in the cells. No, they were not putting us in for good! We changed into the dry clothes taken from our good backpacks, had some food, and tucked ourselves into the blankets provided by our jailkeepers. In the morning they served us breakfast. It was very good. In return we demonstrated our drills, sang some Russian songs, and this time we marched off at the sound of the bugle. Everyone was delighted.

This reminds me of our similar drill demonstration on the Quais of Cannes the year before, in front of a French navy submarine. The sailors came to watch our drills, and the captain invited us to view the sub. That was a really amazing experience. Amazing also is the fact that we teenagers managed to come in contact with the French army, navy, border patrol, and police department, all unplanned by us. Someone had to be planning it, thus taking away all fear or apprehension of these guardians of society.

Colonial Exposition

Meanwhile the city of Paris was planning a spectacular *Exposition Coloniale* for the following year. Mother got a humble but well-paying job with their sanitation department, and we moved to the edge of the *Bois de Vincennes* where the exhibits were being built. For this we moved again, and our apartment was only two blocks from a back gate to the Exposition.

The high school was also close by, and for the first time I remained three years in the same place. I loved school and cried every year when it ended. I brought home honor certificates and a bag full of books earned as prizes.

The *Exposition Coloniale* opened, and I had a free pass because of mother's work. What an extraordinary development in my life. It was the experience of the world being spread at my feet by my unseen Teacher. It was an astonishing display of transplanted villages and small sections of towns from the four corners of the earth; every continent was represented by every color and race. Entire families came to live in their native villages, attending to their normal lives and activities. Even their animals were there, from chickens and goats to camels and elephants and everything in between in their respective habitats. Some were in the wide open spaces; and others under the trees of the *Bois de Vincennes*. People of antipodes met. It was a veritable kaleidoscope of humanity, of customs, of arts and crafts, of music and of cooking. The smells imbued the air from pungent to delectable.

Bewildered tourists swarmed the Cambodian palace, the Nigerian or Zulu huts, and the Taj Mahal, whose half-size replica enthralled the people, especially at night when it was illumined with green floodlights and looked like a transparent emerald. But the real jewels were in the pavilion of the Netherlands, which had an incredible display of precious stones and wealth from their colonies. In the evenings, as the lights dazzled the scenes, you could see many dance performances from ballet to Balinese to belly dancers. At the North African bazaar, *the suq*, the Arabs were busy selling their merchandise, their trinkets and souvenirs. Illustrated volumes *would* be needed to introduce one to the wealth and brilliancy of that multi-cultured world exhibit. I have never seen anything that can compare with it, and it can never be repeated, for the French colonies have all become independent nations, some for better, some for worse.

There was no need of my going to the summer camp while a vacation around the world was two blocks from home. What a wondrous tribute to our Creator this exhibit really was. Man was only able to display His handiwork!

Parade

One lasting impression which paralleled the *Exposition Coloniale* was a 14th of July French Independence Day Parade along the *Champs Elysées*, stretching from the *Place de la Concorde* to the *Place de 1'Etoile*.

Place de 1'Etoile with the Arch of Triumph was started by Napoleon, who intended to ride through it victoriously with his troops after his European conquests. Instead he met his Waterloo and died in disgrace on the isolated island of St. Helena off the coast of Africa. Another emperor finished the building of the Arch.

To me this parade was a demonstration of the crowning glory of the French colonial empire. It proved to be the spark of glory before the fall of the grand but dominating colonial empires lost through the rise of independence.

Meanwhile, what a tremendous show of conquest and pride the parade was. The air was reverberating with wind instruments playing triumphant and victorious marches to troops of foot soldiers in vibrant array representing the colonized nations. Selected companies of soldiers marched with their own leaders and banners with a French flag at the head, all keeping in step. The uniformity and unity was startling, even though only a show.

There were few mechanized units in those days. Apart from a few convertibles with the president, generals, and high officials, there were some tanks, some trucks drawing cannons, and horse-drawn vehicles with smaller cannons, machine guns, cannonballs, and other war supplies. All struck a dull, dark note, a sad reminder of World War I. But the passing sadness dissipated quickly.

There was a pause in the parade, followed by the festive sight of regiment after regiment of cavalrymen on prancing horses pounding the granite stone pavement and foaming at the bit from impatience. Each regiment had horses of matching color, either gray or bay, chestnut or white. *Les Gendarmes,* the police, mounted jet black horses whose rumps were combed in a checkerboard pattern and glistened in the sun.

The horses made quite a show, but even more so their riders in their varied uniforms, some elegant, some unusual, others striking or startling. The French regimental officers from St. Cyr and the Polytechnic School were elegant; the Arabs were unusual, pale as death in their white *burnus*, blanket-like-capes, on their dappled Arabian chargers. The black Senegalese were striking in their gray-blue uniforms and white capes lined in red, undulating in the breeze. The fierce appearance of the battle-wearied French Foreign Legion with desert parched faces and glazed eyes was startling. There may have been a few Bedouins from the Exposition, wrapped in black burnus, showing only eyes, peering at the crowds lining the Boulevard.

There is so much more to say of this assortment of men and horses, of helmets and casks, of swords and scimitars, of rifles and bayonets, parading seemingly peacefully before our eyes, all saluting as they passed the grandstand. Yes, the day has been promised when swords are beaten into plowshares, but that time was not yet. Already my invisible Master was introducing me to the nations of the world, leaving me a taste for something bigger than my high school friends. I became interested in historical and political events and asked the questions, "Who makes and breaks the nations anyway?" I was then in my teens. The answers began to come some thirty years later.

8

Some Fun, Some Work, Some Study

I do not want to go on without mentioning my social life. My favorite pastime was getting together with my school friends for walks and talks, then knitting or crocheting sweater after sweater. Yarn was very cheap, and as a result I was well dressed in spite of our dire condition.

The boys' high school was around the corner, a block away, but we were not interested in boys. Is this against your concept? What, not interested in boys? Not at seventeen and eighteen, not in Paris? No! There were *sorties* with my school pals to the old Trocadero, which was a theater and movie house that could seat five thousand. You can well imagine the raucous noise of that many teenagers coming to see Laurel and Hardy and the like. All were silent movies (not so silent with all of us around) with the piano player dubbing in the sound effects (with our help!).

I also joined a girls' basketball club, and our coach decided to train us in skiff rowing as well. We were the first girls' team to row on the River Seine running through Paris.

A few times in the winter the Russian nobility organized elegant balls. I went twice with two outstanding escorts. The first one, whom I knew through the Russian Scouts, was now an officer of St. Cyr, the "West Point" of France. He came for me in his flashy uniform, white chamois gloves and plumed helmet. My dress was a beautiful pink crepe georgette from the renowned designer Lanvin (even though a hand-me-down from the American girls). I was seventeen. We probably made a striking entrance. As for me, I was oblivious to it all, being neither impressed nor caring to show off, even though I had found out that I had the title of Baroness.

My second dress was of white chiffon with a raspberry red velvet jacket, my mother's creation. My second escort, also in uniform, was French, from the elite school of the *École de Politechniques*, the "M.I.T." of France. I met him at my first ball and saw him often after that. We were good friends, and we both liked to dance. I had no other interest.

The boys and girls from the Scouts were growing up, and we also socialized, meeting in sweet gatherings at some of the parents' apartments. Often I danced most of the night and then played basketball or rowed down the river the next day. My body, especially my shoulders, were so developed that mother asked me if I would choose to be a lady or make football my career. Those were fun years.

The summer after graduation, a distant relative, Madame Bour, decided I should work and she found me a job caring for the children of the *Procureur Général,* the Attorney General. And so, the Procureur, his wife, three children, and myself packed into a car and drove to the mountains of Auvergne, in central France, where they had a vacation home. I did not know what to do with the children, but I could help in the kitchen. Potatoes were grown around there, and we had potatoes every day. On my day off, I skipped on the hilltops covered with purple heather, and stopped to chat at an occasional farm house where I would always be offered a drink and food. Once I came across a golden wheat field swaying in the breeze as a gentle sea. I stopped; a mystical feeling came over me, a feeling of the eternal. I stood for a moment as if in a trance, and it was marvelous. Then it left. I could not explain this experience and told no one about it.

Something else happened that summer which was not pleasant. I felt as if a thin veil was being drawn over my mind. I was losing my acuity for the subjects I had been best in, science and math. It seemed as if the sharpness of my mind was gone. This made me very uneasy as I did not understand what had happened. I never told anyone about this change. Today, I can attribute this dullness to allergies, particularly to potatoes! Even so, my ever present Treasure did not allow this ill feeling to alter my future which He was designing.

Upon my return to Paris, I was faced with the dilemma of how to continue my schooling. The tuition at the Sorbonne was out of reach, and after the beclouded experience in Auvergne, I knew I wouldn't excel at such a highly academic institution.

The same lady, Madame Bour, who found me the childcare job in Auvergne, was the main financial supporter of a private college for social studies, for training social workers, visiting nurses, and Montessori kindergarten teachers. Sister Montessori, an Italian nun, developed and introduced the method in the 1920's. Madame Bour talked my mother into putting me through that college.

Those were sort of dull and uneventful school years, mostly because I was confronted with a side of human life I knew nothing about. That was the point. School is to teach you what you should know, but don't. I knew little about families and their problems, about family laws, first aid, psychology, psychiatry, or pedagogy. It was unreal to me and boring. A Montessori kindergarten was attached to the school where I worked for my keep. Eventually, I did make heart to heart contact with the children and became at ease with these unpredictable little creatures. Poor me and poor them! They had to listen to my off-key singing. Fortunately, some did know the proper tune. The rest of the activities turned out fine. The method worked very well.

Seeds were sown during those two years of college. As the seeds matured, they kept supplying me with common sense. A number of courses were given at the Sorbonne, such as speech therapy, working with mentally handicapped children, and psychiatry. It took me quite a while to comprehend the meaning of the word psychiatry, let alone differentiate between the thinking of the patient and the thinking of our remarkable professor. While attending the courses at the Sorbonne, and later during my apprenticeship at the library, I became acquainted with the *Quartier Latin*, which is the bustling international university district, mostly unchanged from the time when Latin was the language of the university. On the dark side were gatherings in the opium-smoke-filled rooms and many drinking parties, in which I had no interest. What did hold my interest was classical literature, rather than the detective stories as before. Poetry had already started to grip my emotions during my high school years. However, my particular interest during this time, 1934 and 1935, was in the student political rallies. They often became violent at the instigation of the communists. The rising of Hitler in the background, whose agenda was unknown, added to the historical animosity between Germany and France.

Observing the different political parties, from monarchists to Gaulists to others, I soon concluded that none were worth my time. I did not need to look into communism because of good reasons and bad experiences. I really did not know what I expected. I only knew that I did not find it, for it was not there. Nothing expressed my high and hidden ideals.

Subconsciously I was building up an ivory tower. I had a strong sense of right and wrong, of morality and ethics, ideals I could not express and nobody could penetrate, for the One behind the scene was holding the answer to my quest, directing my likes and dislikes.

During those two years, I had Sundays off, as did Mother, whom Madame Bour also had hired as her live-in housekeeper. Therefore we were able to spend most Sundays together. We enjoyed our time walking and musing through miles of museum halls. She was admiring and appreciative of art. As for me, I was just tagging along (at least in the beginning). At the Louvres, she tried to make me appreciate her favorite Italian masters: Andrea del Sarto, Tintoretti, Raphael, Da Vinci, Michaelangelo, and hundreds of other painters and sculptors of all ages. That place was overwhelming by its size and contents. The headless winged Victory at the head of the steps was very dramatic. She and the armless Venus de Milo became companions as we returned to the museum over and over again. Still, I am not sure that we visited every room of furniture, china, glassware, clothing, and tapestry, not to mention the mummies. Nevertheless, I received a solid base in art education through my mother's guidance. Had you asked me what I liked the best, I would have said the smaller, more intimate museums of Cluny, Rodin, the St. Chapelle, and the veiled women statues of the *Jardin des Tuileries*. Amazing how the sculpture could render the impression of a thin veil over the distinct features of a woman's face, in stone!

Mother also introduced me to classical music at the Salle Pleyel. The first time I listened to it, I was bored. The second time, I showed enough interest to want to return. Eventually, I developed a great appreciation for what my generation calls "good music"—Bach, Brahms, Mozart, Wagner, Schumann, Strauss, Bartock, Liszt, Chopin, Debussy, Gounod, Bizet, Massenet, etc. Paris was a living school in every form of art and expression. I learned by living in and through history, brought to life through the arts. *I was in the school of Life, my Treasure was my Teacher.* Epoch by epoch, period by period, style by style, color by color, sound by sound, all became engraved in me.

Consequently, I instinctively know what blends together and what does not. Built into me was a sense of balance and proportion, of harmony and timing, of beauty and appreciation.

On a physical plane, my Wise Master was shaping the earthen vessel— "first the natural, then the spiritual"—while I was unaware of His working to mature me.

9

My First Job

Having finished college as a social worker and Montessori teacher, I found out that my work permit was denied because I was a citizen without a country, even though there was an incredible shortage of social workers. No one, however, could prevent me from working without pay. My aunt, with whom I had lived during my first year in France, was now director of a home for pregnant and unwed mothers and their babies. I was able to work there. My two cousins, Olga and Tatiana, also worked there as nurses. A prominent Greek socialite was president of the home and was very happy to receive my help. My aunt had me sleep in the hall on a pad, which was stored in a closet, but when the Greek woman found out, she gave me a beautiful room in another building overlooking the garden. Our food was good, but I often vomited after a good meal of meat and potatoes. We still did not know about allergies.

The little children were between two to four years old, with one boy, five, and a girl, six. There were at least twenty of them in one big room. The furniture consisted of two long bleached wooden tables and benches along the window wall. We also had six chamber pots along another wall which the little ones were not trained to use. Crying, squabbling and fighting met me at the door. It was chaos. My cousin Olga, who was still very difficult and haughty, was ashamed enough of the situation to help me, at least in the cleaning up. I was to be with the children from breakfast time until supper, with a two-hour break for lunch. The children's food was passed through an opening from the kitchen. It consisted mainly of bread and hot chocolate for breakfast, soup for lunch, and porridge for supper.

Until my arrival, the children never left the cement floor of this dreary room, although there was a small yard near by. They looked miserable, and they were, for they were desperate for some affection. Their response to care, to story telling, to singing, to rhymes was immediate. Jean, the five year old, was a real help in many ways. The problem was with the six-year-old, Mireille. No one could tame her. I asked her mother, who worked in the kitchen and was able to hear what was going on, if she would allow me to spank her child.

"I don't care if you kill her!" was her desperate outcry.

What a tremendous lesson this experience taught me. I had to spank Mireille with my bare hands the first thing after breakfast in front of all the children ("Oh, but you are not supposed to do that," might be your response; wait until you find out about the outcome). After spanking her, I would take her to a cavelike hole under the house and put a piece of picket fence in front, telling her that she could come out when she decided to be good. She would stay in that cave until lunch time when I called her. This went on for a month. My hand was so sore, but I knew this was no time to give in, although I began to feel like a monster. Lo and behold on the thirtieth day, shortly after I had left her in the cave, she came out and stood at the door, tame as a little lamb. The devil had left her. I just hugged her. The lesson learned was, "Spare not the rod." Children love you for disciplining them. This, of course, was an extreme case. Mireille became my best helper, and Jean was my second. We managed to get some supplies, paper, crayons, scissors, yarn, etc., and everyone participated in decorating the walls, bringing some color and brightness to the place.

Each morning we learned to keep a minute of silence to talk to God. Before long we had a kindergarten and preschool, clean and orderly, with well-behaved children. You see, the daily spanking had a good sobering effect on these little ones. The mothers, the workers, and the president of the home were astonished, and so was I. Later, my feeling was that I had graduated from kindergarten and no longer needed to go back to that kind of work, and so it was.

All was well, except that now, by the end of 1935, at the age of twenty, I needed a paying job to go on with my life. If the French did not want me, by refusing to give me a permit to work, then goodbye! Therefore the best conclusion I could come to was to leave France. The Home president was very understanding and even suggested I apply to the royal court of Greece (because of my noble birth) where they were seeking a French tutor. She gave me the address. I offered my services in a letter, but I sent no references or recommendations, being so inexperienced in such matters. Not surprisingly, I never heard from them.

However, at the same time, I wrote about my plight to my aunt Olga in Vienna, who read my letter to her friends in Czechoslovakia where she was visiting. The lady of the estate responded right away, again because of my birth, asking if I would consider living with them. I would speak French (they were Austrians) and relieve the youngest daughter of her supervisory duties with the servants, since she was getting married. I accepted. While waiting, I returned to my mother in Paris from Marseilles. We waited three months to get my Nansen passport and visa. My status still was that of a citizen without a country!

The dear lady from Czechoslovakia provided for my support during that time.

10

ZDANICE

Another Job—Another Country

This next job was a blessed activity. Ten years had elapsed since my trip from Vienna to Paris. This time the trip was in reverse, Paris to Vienna, to meet my Aunt Olga again. At one time during the trip there was only one middle-aged man in the train compartment. Our conversation was very brief. He asked, "Do you think about God?" My answer was, "No." That was that! I did not respond to the gentle nudging of my true Keeper, the One who thought of me all the time.

At the train station in Vienna, my aunt helped me transfer to another train bound for Brunn, or Brno in Czechoslovakia, a much shorter journey. In Brno I was met by the oldest daughter, Elizabeth, and we were chauffeured to the estate. I remember well what I wore, a beautifully-designed brown wool dress done by mother, her brown coat that she took off her back at the station along with matching hat and gloves. There was not much else in my small suitcase.

The family lived in a castle. The chatelaine received me very warmly and asked me to call her Aunt Lilly. She was a tall, gracious, and generous woman in her fifties. She had three daughters: Elizabeth who was thirty, and lived at home; another who was twenty-eight, married, and lived in Vienna; and the youngest, Trudi, who was twenty-six and engaged to be married. Trudi was the one I was replacing.

The master was an imposing gentleman of large stature whom everyone called Dr. Seidl, his full name being Dr. Erwin Seidl von Hochenfeldern. (He was a Ph.D., probably in engineering.) His parents had bought the castlelike fortress from the Lichtensteins. The original fort had been burned down by the Turks centuries before. It was rebuilt by the Lichtensteins who named it "Steinitz" and was modernized by the present owners.

Zdanice

Steinitz became Zdanice, after the formation of the Republic of Czechoslovakia. The castle was built in the shape of a square with a round tower flanking each corner. It had two stories and an inner court for carriages and cars to turn around in. Most of the ground floor was occupied by village administrative offices and their court. One wing was left for the kitchen and laundry quarters. The living quarters were upstairs. The outside walls were six feet thick, of hewn stone. The inside walls were four feet thick. A hall went about on the inner four sides of the castle, with windows facing the inner court and giving access to all the rooms facing outside.

Elizabeth showed me to my room. It had two doors, one on the hall side of the four-foot wall, the other on the room side. In between was a four-foot hallway space. In the room, beside the regular furniture, all baroque, was a six-foot-high cream-colored tile stove. The wood was fed into the stove and the ashes removed from the hall. All the rooms were thus equipped. What a pleasant and clean heating system! However, what warmed my heart the most was a vase of violets at the bedside. No one had ever given me flowers before! I was deeply touched by Elizabeth's thoughtfulness. She also told me that I could leave my clothes in the four-foot hallway space between the doors and I would find them clean in the morning. That was a big relief as I only had one pair of shoes and another old dress.

Elizabeth was very plain looking and simple. She had studied horticulture and was in charge of the park and the gardeners, working along with them. My duties consisted of coming early in the morning to the kitchen and pantry to meet Aunt Lilly who would write the day's menus: one for the gentry, another for the servants. I would give out the corresponding provisions—salt, sugar, flour, everything needed for one day at a time—and then lock everything up or else the food would be stolen by other servants and workers who would come around to help themselves. Apart from the cook and her helpers, there were two laundry women downstairs and two chambermaids and a butler-chauffeur upstairs. After breakfast I would unlock the linen room and distribute the linen according to the daily need, replace the soiled linens, and record what was brought up from the laundry room. Everything had to be accounted for.

As simple as the chores were, none of them came easily to me because, try as I might, I could not rise up on time, even when I was sent to bed early. I was probably traumatized by all the drastic changes in my life. Still I had time on my hands the rest of the day and was given two puppies to bring up.

"What was I going to do with them?" I wondered. After eight years of convent and boarding school life, I had become totally estranged from my childhood animal friends. The only place to keep the dogs was by the servants' quarters in the kitchen yard. Once or twice a day, I brought them to the park surrounding the castle, and since they were young hunting dogs, they would take off after the first sparrow they saw. Elizabeth would help me round them up.

This was not all. Someone had the bright idea of raising chickens, and since I was the only one available, everyone elected me to hatch the chickens. An incubator was somehow found and brought to me, whereupon it was set up by the servants' quarters. What unexpected new daily household chores I had, or should I say sores! They baffled me. Not many eggs hatched since I kept forgetting to turn all of them regularly under the lamp. To make a sad story short, the few full-grown chickens who managed to grow up were finished off by my hunting dog friends. I did not mind; I even helped eat them.

In the fall, the dogs had grown enough to be trained by the hunter, whose job it was to locate deer in the adjoining forests every morning. After the 4 o'clock *Jause* (tea time), the hunter came with the coachman in a horse carriage to drive Dr. Seidl through the woods to find the deer. Deer often linger around certain places, and they were often attracted by the horses and carriage. Dr. Seidl would sit in a hunter's blind (a hiding spot) up a tree, and when lucky would kill a deer. Anyone was invited to come along. I went almost every time. It was such a healing and relaxing moment. Fall was such a beautiful time of year in the woods. The road was covered with soft leaves and smelled so wonderful. Other times during the year, we would hunt for small game. Dr. Seidl treated me as a daughter and friend. Sometimes, there were hunting parties for small game. There usually were about eight hunters who would shoot the game as they emerged from the bushes, being scared out of hiding by the young village boys brought along to beat the bushes. We would all drive out in large farm wagons. This was an all-day affair with picnic food brought to keep us well fed. The evenings were devoted to music, bridge and good conversation. I enjoyed these men and women of noble character.

Hunting was Dr. Seidl's main hobby, and three of the four walls of the long halls were adorned with dozens of trophies, mounted heads, and antlers to prove it. Interspersed were paintings and memorabilia of the battle of Austerlitz, also called the Battle of the Three Emperors, where Napoleon defeated the Russian Czar and the Austrian Emperor. The old battleground was only a few miles away.

The Seidls were industrialists and kept most of their holdings in coal, textiles, and sugar. However, after World War I, they lost a major portion of the beet fields around the castle because they were parceled off to the peasants of the village. However, the peasants would not cooperate to continue growing sugar beets, which Dr. Seidl had proposed to buy from them to keep the villagers and the sugar factory working. When this plan failed, he dynamited the factory out of frustration. However, another factory twenty kilometers away survived. His business headquarters were also there, and he went to work every morning. He was strict and severe at times. I was one of the few in the family who was not afraid of him, which he appreciated.

To give you an idea of Austrian (German) diligence, order, and frugality, we mended kitchen towels in the drawing room after dinner, while sipping Vermouth or liquors the butler brought in. This family had holdings in the best textile mills, wool, cotton, and linen. These fabrics lasted for years, yet Aunt Lilly would sit and mend with Elizabeth and myself. The other daughters would join in when visiting. However, knitting was Aunt Lilly's favorite evening pastime. The Doctor was well supplied with fine cable-stitched wool socks.

Trudi's wedding was, of course, a gala affair. It was at the town church with the conventional Catholic services, and throngs of villagers showed up. Aunt Lilly was prepared with bags upon bags of candy for children and adults alike.

Since the Seidls were connected to the social life of Vienna, the small but lavish reception in the park of the castle was attended by thirty to forty aristocrats from Vienna. Additionally, one young German tycoon, an eligible bachelor, had been, as I found out later, invited especially for me. I was one of the six bridesmaids, and he was my escort. The matchmaking was a flop, much to the Seidl's disappointment. I was not interested and not even impressed by him nor his distinguished chauffeur, nor his eight-cylinder custom-made Mercedes. That young tycoon! He was in the habit of leaving the choosing of a bride completely to luck! He would spread cards out upon a table and then ask the young woman he might be with at the time to draw a card. Of the four queens, if you drew the Queen of Spades, you were it! I drew the Queen of Diamonds and was saved. He never did marry. Later, he died in the Second World War.

A Marriage of Convenience

Georges, the foreman in the restoration and modernization of the castle was also a forlorn Russian refugee. He helped me during the chicken-hatching and dog-raising misadventures. Later, I would see him on his days off. We became well acquainted and decided to join our fate in marriage. He eventually left the castle when the modernization was finished, and I rejoined him in Uzhorod, Carpatho-Russia. Carpatho-Russia was the eastern province of Czechoslovakia, the other two provinces at that time were Slovakia and Bohemia. Later I joined him there and we were married. It was a marriage of convenience. My visa was expiring and I had no place on this earth to go. Being a man, he had been able to obtain Czechoslovakian citizenship. I also thought that two intelligent people could talk over problems and differences and come to agreements. I was wrong. Where was my Treasure?

Georges was fourteen years older than I. I inherited his Czech citizenship and received a bona fide passport the day my visa expired. I was no longer a citizen without a country! After a traditional Russian Orthodox ceremony and dinner at a friend's house, Georges informed me that I had to earn my own living since he did not intend to support me. I swallowed hard, stunned by such a remark, as I was already earning more than he on my job as a French tutor. I had nothing to say. I had sealed my fate; and now I had to pay the consequences. "*Noblesse oblige.*"

Uzhorod was a strange town with a strange mixture of nationalities. The officials and white collar workers were Czech, the business people were Hungarian and Jewish, while the Carpatho-Russians were the workers and peasants. The Gypsies, who traveled throughout Europe during the warm months, spent the winter in Uzhorod. They delighted us with their singing violins and their Czardash dances while secretively "gleaning" all they could from us. Everyone spoke three to four languages, though few could read or write. Located at an important crossroad, Uzhorod was a gateway between east and west, north and south.

Hotels and restaurants took advantage of the foreigners by doubling their prices. I noticed it in the restaurant when Dr. Seidl visited me on his way to hunt in the Carpathian mountains. I spoke of it to Georges, who had worked in tourism in Switzerland. Why not have a tourist bureau? As I was tutoring the wife and daughter of the vice-president of the province, I presented the case to him. He became very interested and promised to introduce the idea to the government in Prague. Price gouging was unacceptable, and welcoming the foreign dignitaries *de passage* would be very constructive. Prague responded very positively, and the vice-president returned with a portfolio. Georges was hired on the condition that I would accompany him when receiving visitors as guests of the government on sightseeing tours. Georges was given an office at the entrance of a new five-hundred-room government office building. He received a car, a camera, and the assistance of the Police Department, who kept account of foreign visitors, because all foreigners had to register. Between the two of us, we spoke Czech, Russian, German, French, Hungarian and English and understood a few more languages. The price gouging was stopped, and many important dignitaries were welcomed. This was to last only a few months.

11

Prague and the Nazis

The year was 1938. Hitler had started his devastating move. First came the occupation of Austria, and then Hungary. The Hungarians in our town, Uzhorod, were very upset, and wanted their independence from Czechoslovakia, for Uzhorod was originally a Hungarian town, when part of the Austro-Hungarian empire. They took advantage of the German occupation in Hungary, wanting to join with occupied Hungary, rather than remain in Czechoslovakia. Great trouble was brewing, and I knew fighting in Uzhorod was inevitable; my inner Guide was at work. "Leave" was His directive. I asked Mother, who had come to be with us a few months earlier, to leave with me, but she would not. Georges wanted me to leave also, so I took the train alone to return to the Seidl's. The street fighting in Uzhorod started before I arrived in Zdanice. Civil war spread throughout the whole city. The small and inexperienced Czech army contingent in Uzhorod was helpless. All they could do was to protect the officials in their retreat. Georges helped in the evacuation. He rejoined me in Brno, Slovakia a month later. Mother again would not come with Georges. She took over my French tutoring job until there were no more students, as families fled. We didn't understand at that time why Mother would not come with us; later, we would understand.

We rented a furnished room in Brno and waited—by that time, all of Europe was in a turmoil. What should we do next? Where could we find a job? Not willing to waste the time, I took English courses at the Berlitz school. Georges wrote letters to look for a job, but there was nothing. Over a month went by. We read the papers, which carried gruesome news, and slept a lot. We did not know what to do.

Then a letter came from Switzerland. A friend of Georges' advised him to check with the United States Consulate in Prague, which was looking for a multilingual receptionist. Georges was tailor-made for the job, and we moved to a small apartment hotel at the edge of Prague in January 1939.

Hitler's plan to exterminate the Jews was in full fury in Germany. Jews were being rounded up and sent to concentration camps. Dachau was in full operation. Those who had not been apprehended were storming the consulates of Europe. The United States consulates were focal attractions, a powerful magnet of hope for those who could escape. In Prague, between three hundred to six hundred applications were processed daily. Jews came from all over Europe.

Because of the occupation of Austria, the air was charged with a dark foreboding. The normally gay Viennese took on somber looks and exchanged their friendly greeting of *Grüss Gott* (God greets you) with *Heil Hitler,* raising their arm. The British Prime Minister, Neville Chamberlain, with his trademark black umbrella, was traveling periodically to Berchtesgaden at Hitler's request.

Everyone felt very uneasy and on the alert when the Czech president Hacha was invited to Berchtesgaden. We asked ourselves, Could we be next? We waited, ears glued to the radio, ready to fight if our turn came. Well, it came, not to fight, but to abdicate!

Orders were given to remain calm, not to provoke, not to retaliate, but to cooperate as the German troops peacefully occupied the land. What? How could that be? Unbelievably,

President Hacha (whose name became "Ha, ha" —a laughing stock) handed over the country with its army to Hitler on a silver platter. People were incensed.

The majority of people stayed home as the troops of the Third Reich marched from the outskirts of town to the center, to the beloved Vaclavske Plaza. March 15, 1939, was Prague's day of mourning. I took a streetcar (empty of all but a few people) downtown, which slowly made its way through the troops. The sidewalks were empty. The silence was broken by the rhythmic pounding of the boots on the pavement. Soon the whole town would smell like cod liver oil from those boots. We hated them.

On the Plaza, a few Czech men on the sidewalks were bold to shout obscenities, booing and spitting in the soldiers' faces, who never blinked an eye. It was all eerie, gloomy, and unreal. What was going on? Where was our army? Within a couple of days the takeover was complete. All government offices were in Nazi hands and the citizen registration started. The main reason for the registration was to find Jews; however, the process was humiliating to everyone because all had their ID's or passports stamped with "Citizen of the Great Thousand-Year German Reich." Now we all became second-class citizens. This was an outrage. Czechoslovakia was probably the best-organized, most orderly, and prosperous democratic country in Europe, even though only twenty years old. The army was small, but modern and strong.

The United States did not officially recognize the occupation, and the United States Consulate was cautiously watchful. Their work was intensified, trying to handle all the applications of the desperate people.

I began to feel very restless in Prague and went to visit my friends, or should I say my adopted relatives, the Seidls. We all went to Vienna to see their occupation for ourselves. People were greeting one another with the "*Heil Hitler*" pantomime to which I would respond, "*Grüss Gott.*" Aunt Olga and grandmother Schwachheim were still there. It was to be my last visit with them. At seventy-eight Grandmother had not lost an ounce of her dignity, still wearing her hair up and a black velvet ribbon around her neck. Poverty only strengthened her character. Five years later they were to flee again from the Russian allied troops (the Communist Red Army) as they overran Austria with their tanks, their motorized units, and their unruly drunken soldiers. The last I heard was that they had gone to Linz, on the Danube river in eastern Austria.

What about the Communists? They were not yet a threat in 1939, not even on the apparent horizon. Besides, they had signed a pact of nonaggression between Ribbentrop and Molotov. Still something was stirring in me again. Something or Someone was telling me that they would come. A feeling of uneasiness was over me, and I did not want to be around when they would come. The name Baroness von Schwachheim was not a threat to the Germans, but there was no chance of survival for a White Russian under the Communist Red Army regime.

"Go to America!"

By September 1939, while Poland was being ruthlessly bombed, I told Georges that I was fed up with Europe, its wars, and its revolutions. No government was worth fighting for, anything would be better than staying in Europe. I would rather go and climb trees with African pygmies. He reported my remarks at work and the United States Consul offered to give me an affidavit, a statement of support, and said, "I know you will take care of yourself and not be a charge to the United States government." He would vouch for me. The visa was easy to obtain since the Russian quota was wide open. I could migrate to America, although I knew little about it. Europe did not relate much to the New World then, so whether I would go and climb trees or shoot Indians, what would be the difference? Anything would be better then Europe. The Consul assured me that there were also well-educated and cultured people in the States. I thanked him kindly through Georges, who acted as my intermediary. I didn't make a decision right away.

A few days later, in the middle of the night, I was awakened by a decisive and authoritative inner voice, "*Go to America!*" I awakened Georges and told him that my mind was made up to go to America and that I would accept the visa and affidavit offered by the Consul. I attributed this inner voice to my clever subconscious mind, compiling and deciding. I still did not know any better. No one had ever told me that God could speak to people. What a loving Father I had.

"Though thy way be long and dreary, eagle strength He'll still renew;

Garments fresh and feet unweary, tell how God hath brought thee through."

After the initial occupation, people were ordered to go back to work. They lived in silent fear of the Nazi-enforced blackouts, but at the onset of darkness a dense crowd would gather on Vaclavske Plaza to sing the Czech national anthem and other national songs well into the night. From the rooftops, the Nazi guards would shoot at random into the crowds, occasionally wounding or killing someone. However, from among the students, two to three demonstrators were executed every morning.

Where we were now living was only two blocks away from the nightly demonstrations. Every night at suppertime friends would show up to listen to the British Broadcasting Company from London. Radio Prague was only barking commands at the population—no news. Of course, to listen to the B.B.C. was *verboten*. We made sure that the doors and windows were locked, and we covered up the telephone with pillows. Many phones had been wiretapped. No one could afford to be caught. How would you explain such a gathering of friends, if caught? Who could understand that there was a bond deeper than nationality? We were friends: a Czech, Germans, Russians, Jews, an Armenian who kept us in stitches with his hilarious monologues, and then a retired captain of the British Navy. He would disappear regularly for a week or so, to reappear and tell us what went on in London!

He amazed us. He was not an official spy, he was only doing his duty for his country.

Food rationing had begun, one egg a week, etc. This did not concern us yet since we could eat our dinner at midday without rations in the restaurants. In the evenings we all pulled together our resources and eggs while listening to the news; then we would go off to the demonstrations. We sneaked out of the apartment carefully, one or two at a time, and went to be lost in the crowd on Vaclavske Plaza. Being young, I liked the excitement.

However, I would not be staying in Prague much longer. I was going to America! Much preparation was required. It took a month to contact what seemed to be a dozen government departments, assembling all sorts of documents—rent bills, police clearance, financial statements. The most difficult were the birth certificate and marriage license which were in Uzhorod with the Hungarians. All I had had was the Nansen passport until I received my Czech passport. At that time I was given an official, but derived, birth certificate, given on the basis of the Nansen passport

To receive a permit, we needed to prepare a declaration of intent to leave the country as tourists. Georges asked, "Can I please come along?" I told him, "If you will come along, then you will have to support me!" Well, he came but did not support me, at least not while he was alive. The irony of it is that today I am collecting half of his Social Security check. While Georges did not live up to his marital responsibilities, after his death, my righteous God would not let me be cheated the rest of my life.

The American visas and affidavits were on separate documents since the German passports of the Thousand Year Great German Reich were not considered valid. I also needed special permits to take out jewelry, cameras, fur coats, three transatlantic trunks of clothes and linens, and some money. The Nazis had all but stopped tourist travel. Only Jews were allowed to leave, with little more than the clothes on their backs and fifty dollars cash. I had to fight for my rights. Not being Jewish, why should I be given the same treatment? I fought like a tiger, strengthened by the inner speaking, *"Go to America!"*

Dr. Seidl had come to Prague to be interviewed by high-ranking German officials who needed his help both as an industrialist and as a host to introduce other Czech industrialists to the Germans. We had dinner together a couple of times, and I told him of my plans to leave Europe and asked him for some introductions and recommendations, specifically concerning my being politically neutral and harmless. His help was a major factor in my release.

It was very magnanimous on Dr. Seidl's part to help me leave when actually he wanted to keep me close by and protect me. My allowance, since my days in the castle, had kept coming through all of these years. He felt it was unfair that I had lost my family's inheritance and offered to buy me a small castle by a lake in the Tyrol Mountains! Incredible! But it was a dream I could not accept. The inner voice was compelling me to leave, and I begged him also to leave and take Aunt Lilly to Switzerland, where they had a small bank account.

"Why?" he asked.

"Because the Russian Red Army will come."

It sounded too farfetched for anyone but me to believe. Through my foresight I knew the Communists would come. *If only they had listened!*

Twenty years before, I was pleading with my family to leave Russia, and now I was pleading with my friends, "Leave Czechoslovakia." This was more than premonition; it was a divine speaking, a prophetic speaking from my Treasure. *If only they had listened.*

While in Prague, Dr. Seidl had dinner with the general in charge of the occupation, who told him that the Czech army was extremely well equipped and prepared, well beyond Hitler's evaluation. Had they fought, it would have given the Nazis a crucial and crushing blow; instead, an entire arsenal was handed over to them. Why did President Hacha turn over his country to the enemy? Why? So many unanswered why's. I asked myself again, Who is making and breaking the nations?

Having collected all of the necessary documents into a portfolio, I turned them over to the proper authorities and was told to wait three weeks. During these three weeks, there was time to visit the Seidl's once more in Zdanice and receive a going-away present: yardage of woolens, cottons, and silks which I had made into coats and suits and dresses before I left, a ten-year supply. When Aunt Lilly and Dr. Seidl took me to the train station to return to Prague, I quickly boarded, so as not to lose my composure, but when I went to the window to shake their hands for the last time, I broke out in a torrent of uncontrollable tears. I sensed that I would never see them again. I was ashamed that they had done so much for me while I had done nothing for them. Yet had they listened to my pleading, they could have averted so much devastation and ruin.

Three weeks had elapsed, and I retrieved my portfolio and marched to the Nazi Headquarters to see the Gauleiter (the one in charge of the country). Lastly, I needed his approval. While waiting in line at the information desk I noticed the attitude and the speaking of the young Nazi clerks. They were provoking, arrogant, and rude. In front of me, a little old lady in a kerchief, all hunched up and trembling, asked a simple question and received a barrage of insults. Standing behind her I could not keep silent: "You should be ashamed of yourself, treating an innocent person like a dog."

My unexpected boldness silenced them for a moment, then they asked, "Who are you?" For the first time in my life I used the title that impressed even the Nazis.

"I am Baroness von Schwachheim, and I came to see the Gauleiter."

"The Gauleiter is out of town." This was a fabulous arrangement by my silent Guardian.

"Then let me see the next in command." A phone call was made, a very short answer given, and I was told to follow two armed S.S. guards. Me? Between two S.S. troopers? It hit my funny bone. This was ridiculous. It reminded me of an opera. I could not take it seriously, but of course I did not show it.

I was introduced. The soldiers were dismissed, and the Vice-Gauleiter read my name again. His name also ended in "-heim". We were countrymen, from Bavaria. This opened the way for a normal conversation, for a few platitudes, and then came the question:

"Why do you want to leave? Don't you like it here?"

I had to think fast. I could not answer, "No, I don't like it." Instead I said, "All my life I have traveled from country to country. Now I want to see America. I am tired of wars and revolutions. After fifteen years of being a citizen without a country, I finally received a citizenship and a nice passport. Two years later you came and invalidated it and stamped it "Citizen of the Great One Thousand Year German Reich," making me a second-rate citizen; and how long will this last?" I paused. Then I kept talking; I could not help myself, "You are building an Eiffel Tower without nuts and bolts." It was a thunderous and lightning statement. Was this another one of my spontaneous predictions? It proved to be so five years later when Paris was liberated and the Nazis' Thousand Year Reich collapsed.

The Vice Gauleiter shifted in his armchair, looked at me perplexed, and said, "*Gnädige Frau* (reverent lady), I beg you not to speak this way. It could get you into great trouble." I was quiet, very quiet. He glanced at and signed my papers, called the guards and handed me my portfolio. Nothing more was said. I was dismissed. Whew!

No good looks, no title, no fellow-countryman, could claim to have spared me. It was the One standing at my side who had better intentions for me than to see me shot at sunrise.

We were free to leave Prague! My last recollection was of an episode with the egg that I had redeemed with my ration in the morning. I had carried it ever so carefully in my handbag all day to give to someone. This person turned out to be a very grateful porter at the train station that night. It gave me a sense of achievement! We made one last attempt to persuade Mother to come with us, but again, she declined.

How was this trip financed, you may ask? Amazingly enough, it was by some Jewish acquaintances we had helped along the way. When they left the country, they preferred to give us their money rather then to turn it over to the Nazis. The loving Master Planner provided for everything, beyond all I could ask or think, and I took it all for granted.

12

The Journey

There are times in life when it is better not to think, for you cannot change anything. One must not look back and develop a heartache, nor look forward and become anxious. One must just quietly and carefully handle every moment.

After the sweet goodbyes to friends and the egg episode at the train station, we entered into a ghostly world, dimly lit. The signs *Schweigen* and *Verboten* could barely be read because it was so dark. Our train car was almost empty. In our compartment two men by the window had already settled down, their hats pulled over their eyes. The train rolled through the dark night. There was not a flicker of light, for the blackout was total. I was restless and went walking up and down the corridor. A German soldier in a green uniform (the S.S. wore black) came out of his compartment. We started talking in a whisper. He invited me to his compartment to join his four companions. We were about the same age, talking and laughing about nothing, and forgetting about politics and war. Our party did not last long. An S.S. officer, peering in, ordered me out. Fraternizing was *verboten*.

As we entered the plains of Germany, the moon rose over a fright-provoking landscape. Nothing but tanks, motorized vehicles, artillery, and planes lined both sides of the tracks for hundreds of kilometers. Shattering!

We stopped briefly in Berlin. The two gloomy passengers in our compartment left, and another one with a friendly, open face came in. At daybreak we started talking. He was a Dutch businessman with chocolate brown eyes. We laughed at small jokes and he presented Georges and me with a box of Dutch chocolates! We did not want to eat any before Hamburg where we planned to get off the train and have a snack. In Hamburg we ordered food, and were asked, "Where are your rations?"

"What rations? Restaurants were not rationed in Prague." There was a big commotion, and people were upset at hearing that. "You need coupons to order restaurant foods here." No coupons, no food. No one had warned us. The chocolate would now have to last us until Holland, but we had no complaints!

The kind businessman gave me a crash course in the Dutch language, showing me the similarity with the German language, both from the same root. He taught me how to read and how to listen. This was a tremendous help. During our three days in Holland, I could read and understand much. I answered in German and was understood. However, we were not at our destination yet.

At the border, gloom and doom increased. The atmosphere was mournful. S.S. border officials in black appeared in the poorly lit room, barking orders and demanding our passports and papers, then disappeared behind closed doors while our hearts sank. No one spoke. The room was overflowing, mostly with Jews. Everyone was in suspense, frozen.

"Don't think!" I remembered to take my own advice. Today I would say, "Let go and let God!" Finally a couple of S.S. men came towards us. We held our breaths. They handed us our papers: "You are released to go." We walked quickly toward the Dutch guards with a sigh of relief.

The date was November 22, 1939, my birthday. I was twenty four, and we were in Rotterdam. And, oh, the food! For breakfast alone we were served six kinds of everything: six kinds of cheeses, six kinds of cold cuts, six kinds of jams and honeys. There was fruit, eggs, bread and butter, and coffee, tea, and hot chocolate. The stores were jammed with goods. The fruit and vegetable markets were spilling over on the sidewalks. Life was vibrant, bustling with enormous activity.

We spent only three short nights in the hotel, sleeping little, for there was just too much to see. The efficient, clean, and fast electric trains were running to all parts of the country, carrying us here and there. Of course, being of Russian descent, we went to the Zuiderzee where Peter the Great learned how to build dikes and ships in his youth. I was very impressed by this Dutch village built mostly of two-story red brick houses with white trim and A-shaped roofs. They were all alike, with three steps leading to the door, and they looked so neat with their white curtains behind sparkling clean windows. The narrow streets were paved with bricks which were washed down with soap and water every morning by the housewives. Such thorough cleaning also kept the sea salt from corroding the bricks.

We were among the last tourists to enjoy the beauty of old Rotterdam. Days later the border was closed. There was to be no more travel. Shortly after, Holland was invaded, and during those terrifying years of war, Rotterdam was bombed and razed to the ground.

In Prague, we had booked passage on the *New Amsterdam*. As we boarded the ship and glided out of port, a deep sense of relief, a *joie de vivre*, overtook me again, an experience I had not had for a long time. I had made contact with my inner self. I was going to America! From where did that sense of security come? Was it not from my Treasure?

The other passengers, who were ninety-nine percent Jewish, were so worried, so anxious, and so concerned, when they should have been rejoicing because of having escaped the Nazis and Europe. Now, their fears came from the troubled sea because the ship had to sail very slowly through numerous mine fields. The English Channel was mined by the Dutch, the Belgians, and the French along one shore, by the British along their shore, and by the Germans in the middle. Sailors stood on deck with long,

long canes watching for mines twenty-four hours a day. When they did see a mine, they would gently push it aside. It took us five days instead of one to arrive at the open sea.

From the white cliffs of Dover to Southampton where more passengers boarded, we kept close to the British coast. Skeletons of blown up ships kept reminding us of the danger of our voyage. There also were U-boats, lurking for their prey. At night, the *New Amsterdam* was fully lit to give a clear signal that we were a passenger ship, not a warship.

Many were seasick; the dining room had fewer and fewer patrons. I, on the other hand, felt good. I ate well, enjoying the delicious gourmet food. Most of my time was spent on deck in my new fur-lined tweed coat and felt boots, reading a big fat book on Alaska, given to me by Dr. Seidl. People surmised that I was sailing to Alaska to claim my inheritance. Far from it. My inheritance was my inner secret, a Treasure that kept me on an even keel, whether I acknowledged it or not. I did not acknowledge it then.

On its return trip, the *New Amsterdam* was empty of passengers, having only its crew members. It hit a mine and blew up in the Channel. What horror! It was very sad.

13

America

My First Impressions

On December 5, 1939, the New York harbor was overloaded with passenger ships bringing refugees from Europe. The *New Amsterdam* had to dock in Hoboken, New Jersey. There was so much hustling about that I do not remember where we went through immigration; it could have been Staten Island. I was only interested in getting off the ship. At the pier an American met us. He had been a co-worker of Georges at the Embassy. Georges had made a deal with him while in Prague to secure U.S. dollars for us when we would arrive in America. The American kept his monthly pay at the State Department in Washington D.C., while Georges paid him a monthly stipend in Czech crowns. This was money Georges primarily was receiving from some Jews who were giving him their money rather than to the Nazis. This was done in exchange for the help Georges gave them with their visas.

The American consular official came to bring us the money and help us find a furnished room close to the Holland Tunnel. Hoboken was a dismal place, nothing but brick, cement, rusty iron, asphalt, and smoke. We were close to a high school, and the teenagers wore heavy white socks. They looked sloppy to me. I found out they were wearing bobby socks, a famous fad.

We went to Manhattan every day and moved there the following week.

My three weeks of English instruction by an Englishman did nothing to help me understand the people in New York City. Even Georges had trouble. Their accent was so different, but we met smiling and helpful people.

There were no police checks at every turn. It was a striking contrast from Europe. The atmosphere was easy and free. You could sense it in the air. Liberty is a condition you can breathe. My reaction was, "I don't know what this country is all about, but it is for me. I like it. This is God's country!" I went to apply for my citizenship at the end of the first week in the States, and so did Georges.

Mother would not come with us, not to Prague, not to the States. She remained in Uzhorod during the street fights and then went to Budapest. She wrote us a card while we were in Prague asking us to visit and greet her cousin Boris in New York, who was a brother to Nadia and Georges of the *Consommateur de Pétrole* in Paris.

We visited him, his wife, and in-laws. He offered us hospitality until we could find a place. We stayed only a few days because Georges had some leads from his colleagues at the consulate and quickly found a job as a caretaker of a large estate near Port Jarvis and the Delaware River. There was no real work involved; he just walked around the grounds with the shotgun he had bought at Abercrombie and Fitch on Fifth Avenue a few days after our arrival. On this estate, he shot ducks, geese, crows, and squirrels. We also fished through ice on the pond.

This was a relaxing and healing time for my soul, which needed the peaceful surroundings of nature. I took long walks, studied English a little, knitted, read, and enjoyed our new two-bedroom log cabin, the caretaker's lodging. The best help for now was not to think about the past nor speculate about the future.

While still in New York, Georges sold a few of my things, including my precious Roliflex camera, the only thing of value I owned, without even asking me. What nerve! I was shocked and hurt, but then he bought a one-year-old black Buick sedan with 23,000 miles on it at a price of four hundred dollars. It was such a good deal that I could no longer complain.

"Job Well Done"

We lived on the property through the summer of 1940 and observed some undefined and strange activities. One of Georges' duties every Saturday was to open the windows of the master's big house and welcome a number of club members, all Germans, who came in a dozen or so cars. We could not find out what club this was and became uneasy, knowing they were all Germans. What were they doing in such a remote and wooded place? After a while, we decided to take down their license plate numbers. We thought perhaps they could be useful in the future.

Useful they were! Eighteen months or so later, after Pearl Harbor, Georges and I discussed the secretive activities of the "club members" and we decided to turn over the license numbers I had recorded to the F.B.I.

At the end of the war the F.B.I. sent a word to us, indirectly: "Good job, well done!" A sizable ring of Nazi spies had been uncovered, with its headquarters in New York. It turned out that this gave me a good record with the F.B.I, as, through the years, well-meaning older ladies would turn me in for a spy just because I was Russian-born.

Addressee Deceased

During our time in Port Jarvis, a card I had written to mother was returned "*addressee deceased.*" Bewildered, I read it several times. Could that really be? Checking with others for its meaning, I had to acknowledge that, yes, that is what it meant: dead. Mother had died. Why? How? When? I was too traumatized to even cry, but I thanked God for delivering her from an agonizing life, barely surviving, alone, as a citizen without a country. She must have known that she was very ill, which explained her persistent reluctance to come with us.

After a while, I was restless on the estate, longing to be with more people and improve my English. Georges agreed to leave this position, and so we returned to New York and found a rented furnished room. I began to embroider gorgeous silk underwear for Hollywood stars through the initiative of a Russian refugee who had developed a thriving business. I was earning three dollars a day, which was plenty to eat on. Most fruits and vegetables were ten cents a pound, butter and hamburger were twenty-five cents a pound, and eggs twenty-five cents a dozen. We could even afford strawberries in winter! Gasoline was ten gallons to a dollar. Amazing!

Someone talked me into going to a modeling school: "Go to the best; go to the John Powers School of Modeling." He had the highest reputation. During the interview, Mr. Powers was interested in my cosmopolitan life and my languages. He said my English would improve quickly and the accent was marketable. He wanted to introduce culture amongst his models.

"You have a good bone structure," he said, "Come and get acquainted with the program."

"What kind of financial arrangement do you offer?" I asked.

"We train you and help you find modeling jobs. We ask you to pay ten percent of your earnings to the school."

"Is this to be a life-long arrangement?"

"Yes."

"Ten percent for life regardless of who finds the jobs?"

"Yes."

"No, thank you. I cannot sign such an agreement. Sorry." And I walked out. I am not for sale, I thought. Subsequently, friends found for me a down-scale modeling school that I could attend, and I finished in a month.

Among the acquaintances I had was a young Jewess my age, Georgette, whom I had befriended in Prague. She was beautiful, and with her long blonde hair, she looked like the actress Veronica Lake. I had brought her jewelry to the States. She had given it to me so that she wouldn't have to turn it over to the Nazis when she left Czechoslovakia.

Together we went to the Ansonia Hotel on West 72nd Street to visit one of her acquaintances, where some Jews that Georgette knew had just arrived from Europe. One of them was a surgeon from Budapest. I told him that my family knew the Weiss's, owners of the Czepel Armaments Works, and that my mother had died in Budapest just a few months before. I knew nothing about her death and often wondered about it. We talked about Czepel. He had been working there as a surgeon in their hospital. Then he asked,"What was your mother's name?"

"Hélène Rainaud."

"Wait a moment," he said, recollecting. "Your mother was my patient. Yes, I remember. She had cancer of the uterus. It was too far gone. We could only sew her up and tell her that it was all right to go home and rest." She passed away two weeks later at the age of forty-five.

Is it coincidence that I should meet her doctor and receive firsthand details about my dear mother's death? No! Never! It was in the Father's plan to reassure me and stop my painful wondering. Such was the thoughtful consideration of a merciful God towards a thoughtless creature, a God showing mercy even when we do not recognize Him working behind the scene.

14

Kalamazoo

Georges was busy finding a way to get out of New York. Walking up and down Broadway around 72nd Street, where a good number of Jewish refugees lived, he met up with some of the people who had passed through his desk at the consulate in Prague. He found out that the American Jews had a society helping the newly arrived to get settled in some other city or state. The Protestant Association of Churches was also giving a helping hand to Christian refugees. Georges went to a couple of interviews without telling me and then informed me that we were leaving for Kalamazoo, Michigan. Just like that. I had no choice.

"Kalamazoo! What is that? Where is it?"

After Paris, Vienna, Prague, cities steeped in art and culture, and then New York with the bright lights of Broadway where we had seen "Gone With the Wind," I thought, "What in the world will I do in Kalamazoo?" I was unhappy and pouting en route. There was an inner stirring and a speaking I had not experienced in a long time: "Just follow your husband." It calmed me down. I had heard vaguely that a wife was expected to submit to her husband.

The Buick was performing very well. On the new Pennsylvania Turnpike, Georges was speeding at 85 miles per hour when a lady passed him. She told us at the next gas station that she had been driving 125 miles per hour. I was being introduced to an "America running on a fast track." I liked the speed! What a contrast with the rural life of Carpatho-Russia. You could seldom travel over 40 and had to stop frequently to poke cows and sheep out of the road. It was the end for the chickens if they did not get out of the way.

As we arrived in Kalamazoo, a church committee awaited us and two ladies showed us the apartment they had prepared. The refrigerator and the cupboards were stacked with food. We were astounded at such a warm welcome. Nothing like that ever happened in Europe. A couple of job opportunities were presented to Georges, and he started working for the Allen Electric Company.

Kalamazoo was a friendly town of some 80,000 people in 1940. The women's clubs welcomed me, eager to hear of my experiences. Since my vocabulary was of about 500 words or less, it was often a guessing game with audience participation. This made it quite lively, and I was asked to speak (if you can call this speaking) almost every week and received a generous donation.

I was amazed at how naive, uninformed, or gullible, the American people were. Hitler was taking over Europe, and in the United States soldiers were practicing with rakes and brooms for lack of guns. For one year, I was warning everyone to get prepared for involvement, to get prepared for rationing. Where was I getting such insight? Was it not from my Treasure?

Then came Pearl Harbor! It shook the country to its roots. America woke up and went into high gear, working on the fast track. The Optimists Club invited me to speak. I could only reply that I had nothing more to say as I had already told them of the up-coming involvement in the war.

Time came to look for work. I modeled in the one and only department store, Gilmore's. Soon after, I took care of the style shows, and in-between the shows, I worked in the jewelry department. After a year, I decided to start dressmaking and work for myself.

During the war years I spent the evenings with my ears glued to the radio, catching every commentator possible on every war front, and suffered with the people. The food and gas rationing introduced at the beginning of the war in the States was so generous that it did not even concern me.

I Thought I had a Home

Georges and I worked steadily, and in three years we could put a small deposit on a typical Cape Cod style wood-siding house. The payments were $57 a month. For the first time in my life I thought I had a home. Yes, I thought I had a home. But it was only a house, for my relationship with Georges was so bad, so strained, and we were growing further and further apart. He was a pessimist and had a double personality; I was an optimist, liking people, loving to laugh and to go out. So I went alone. Finally, I decided to go on a prolonged vacation to New York.

In New York, I rented a small room, my gilded cage, overlooking Central Park South, from a very sweet and talented lady. Carol was a concert pianist who presented and performed condensed operas to a mink and sable elite audience at the hotel Pierre or at the Essex House. Often, when coming home from work, I would be met at the door by an operatic aria. It was very refreshing. I liked music and Carnegie Hall was only a couple of blocks away. At the ticket window I became a friendly *habituée*, and the men would tell me, "Do not miss such and such a concert," sometimes giving me a complimentary pass. I attended a concert under the masterful Arturo Toscanini and was allowed to sneak in on one of his rehearsals. I witnessed him stopping the orchestra to tell one of the musicians that he was an eighth note off. Toscanini could detect the slightest wrong vibration among one hundred players. At Carnegie Hall, that winter, I heard many of the best American orchestra conductors.

During the day, I worked as a custom dressmaker for a Russian, Valentina, a popular dress designer of the time. When she made the front page of a national magazine and two of the ladies of Kalamazoo found out that I was executing some of Valentina's designs, they came to the salon and asked for me. This was strictly taboo, for the designs were guarded and we were sworn to secrecy. One of the women was an Upjohn (of the pharmaceutical company). This impressed my employer, and I was called in: "Would you come back to Kalamazoo and design for us?" she asked.

"Yes, maybe later."

Not having a radio, I had stopped listening to news after D-Day. I was appreciating my freedom, my relaxing life, my self. I liked the little sub-basement restaurants around 57th Street and their cuisine, and the daily walks through Central Park to and from work. I was enjoying myself but only to a point. Beyond the horizon was the oppressive reminder of Georges.

In retrospect, I can see how God used him. Unwittingly, Georges guided my life. Because he was Czech, I received the Czech citizenship; because he worked at the U.S. Consulate, the Consul gave me a visa and a personal affidavit; because Georges did not like New York, he accepted help and took me to Kalamazoo.

In Kalamazoo, which in Indian means, "boiling pot," I had been in a pressure cooker. After the first few months, life began rushing upon me faster then I could handle it. I had no control over the events and let them push me around. The American lifestyle was too fast, too demanding. Europe was much more *gemütlich* (cozy).

Often, I became homesick for my European friends. When I was still in New York, I went to the German Consulate inquiring about returning to Europe. "You are crazy *Gnädige Frau*, wait until the war is over!" Yes, I had met a lot of smiling and helpful people, but they were always on the run. There was no time to establish a friendship. I was constrained to follow their lifestyle, which was also on the run. The job, the house, the cooking for a difficult husband, the washing and ironing, all coming at once. I could not handle it. Eventually, I sent out the laundry. On the one hand I was being "cooked," put under pressure, but on the other hand, I learned a great deal in Kalamazoo.

There, I learned English, became Americanized and received my coveted citizenship. I was proud to be an American. To give up my title of Baroness meant nothing. I never used it in the States and only a handful of people knew about it. True nobility is of the character, of the spirit, and no one can put it on or take it away.

My life in Kalamazoo was not over yet. After a few months Georges came to New York to ask me to come back. Because I had a house, even if not a home, I did return. My work was all cut out for me in dress designing and dressmaking. The customers were waiting. I turned the dining room into a workshop. I had bought some yardage in exclusive stores in New York which gave me a start.

I trained a young woman on the job as a finisher. She was a good worker and always on time. One day she announced her engagement, and we made her wedding gown. The wedding was to be in Chicago and she asked for a few days off. "Sure, no problem."

"How did the wedding go?" I asked her when she returned.

"Beautiful. I married the bridegroom's best man!"

"What?"

"We met at the rehearsal and fell in love. The wedding arrangements were all made, the preacher was there, the guests were there—it was a perfect setting. So why wait?"

"What?"

Twice a year I would travel to New York to buy fabrics for my customers who trusted me with money and taste. I would stay with my girlfriend Georgette who always managed to get tickets to the best shows on Broadway. We saw "South Pacific," "The King and I," "Carousel," "Brigadoon"—I do not remember them all, and after the show we went to Reuben's for a midnight snack. Sometimes, she invited friends and we went dancing to the swinging beat of Tommy Dorsey or Guy Lombardo; we had fun. There were no emotional attachments.

However, the emotional void in my life was becoming unbearable. I could no longer cry on Dr. Seidl's shoulder, not even in letters, for he was no more. Dr. Seidl passed away after losing his estate and castle to the Communists. What I had dreaded so many years before had come to pass. As the Red Armies were approaching, he, Aunt Lilly, Elizabeth (their oldest daughter) and the servants who wanted to come along, had put some belongings in two horse-drawn farm wagons and had traveled three weeks to safety, where in a mountain village near Switzerland, he had died. My one trusted friend was gone.

I still did not know that I had a Heavenly Father to comfort me with inner strength. Georges was ever so antagonistic. Nothing I did pleased him. I needed help, someone to talk to, to counsel with on how to handle Georges. One person in the community, whom I knew, seemed to be the right one. Paul was twice my age and had a daughter twenty years old. I was inexperienced enough to hope to establish a fatherly relationship and receive advice. We became friends and soon after Paul fell in love with me. I was shocked at his advances, but my emotional need was greater than my sense of propriety or morality. Actually, Georges's attitude was pushing me into the arms of another. Although I did not solicit such a clandestine relationship, it did make my life bearable for a while. But, deep inside there was a muddy feeling that I covered up.

Jeune Fille

After two years of successful dress designing, I became tired of it, tired of fulfilling the whims of wealthy women. Why not sell ready-made clothes in a boutique? I invited a buyer from the department store to give me the ABC's of a retail store operation. I knew nothing about wholesale, retail, mark-ups, credits and returns. Where would I buy? What brands would I carry? She gave me all the information in one afternoon, in the garden over a cool drink.

Chicago's Merchandise Mart was showing the fall collections. It was May 1948. I visualized immediately what I was going to do. Kalamazoo had two colleges on opposite hills. At the bottom of the hills was a quaint Tudor-type building with several shops. The location was perfect and attractive. When I told the landlord of my intentions and desire to rent a store, he looked at me bewildered. "How did you know that a store will be available in July?" The timing was perfect.

I had one thousand dollars. Five hundred dollars went towards rent, furnishings and the decorations. The decorating consisted of designing the lay-out, the painting of the walls, and the making of draperies, all of which I did myself. The other five hundred dollars went towards merchandise. I paid half cash in advance and obtained immediate credit from my wholesale suppliers. At three, four, and six dollars an item wholesale, the blouses, skirts, slacks, sweaters, jackets, vests, and scarves would make a sufficient showing on opening day. The date was set for August 15, 1948. I called the boutique "*Jeune Fille,*" Young Miss, since it was geared to the college girl.

Having sold two hundred and fifty dollars worth of merchandise the first day, I had to quickly reorder and pay some of the invoices. A month later, I had to borrow one thousand dollars to show a better selection. Mrs. Allen, from Allen Electric, advanced the money, with trust being my only collateral. I repaid it within six months and finished the year with a gross of thirty-six thousand dollars in sales, and an inventory of ten thousand dollars. How about that? It was not bad!

In the Merchandise Marts of Chicago and New York, I was looking for coordinated items, mix and matches, separates and suits. At that time, there seemed to have been only one house on the West Coast that showed what I wanted: affordable clothes, simple, well made with seams finished on the inside, good colors, and attractive to young college students. With mix and matches they could build a versatile wardrobe. I was instrumental in pushing the manufacturers to make more coordinates. They eventually came and still are best sellers.

In summer, as the colleges closed, I moved most of the inventory to Saugatuck, a tourist place on Lake Michigan. Business was very good, partly because of a very energetic young lady who had just turned sixteen. This gave her the right to work and to drive her new red convertible, a birthday present from her parents. She was quite a girl!

My advertising layouts, made on the spur of the moment with the advertising agent, were very appealing and catchy, so he said. People could not help noticing them. The college girls themselves were my public relations department. By asking me to help them with their homecoming float, they advertised for the store. I helped them design the float and furnished the material and the clothes. They received the first prize, even though drenched by a pouring rain.

A college professor in business administration stopped in the store especially to congratulate me. "I can tell by your window displays that you know what you are doing." What he did not know is that I was propelled only by common sense and a built-in education.

My business philosophy was very elementary: Be friendly and honest. Look out for the customers' interest and not the dollar, and they will return. They did. By helping in their selections, the customers appreciated the attention, and the merchandise returns were kept at three percent. I spoke of these returns to one of the wholesalers in New York, expecting to do better in the future. He introduced me to a prominent Chicago buyer who wanted to know my secret, for his returns in a large department store were thirty percent. I answered: "Through personal attention and honesty, I'd rather lose a sale than sell something unbecoming. My policy was: Cash and carry, no credit, closed on Sundays."

The following year, the store being well replenished, I earned a thousand dollars a month. At the end of my second tourist season, I was offered a prime location, excellent for a third boutique.

By the summer of 1950, Georges stopped working, saying that he was tired of working. No, it was not to help me. I had to take the bus to and from work, mow the lawn, shovel snow, and cook, while he went fishing and hunting, bought on credit, and vacationed on my account, not caring for the house or car payments.

At that time, the demanding activities and anxieties of life overran my inner voice and buried my Treasure, giving rise to self-confidence and pride. I could do it all on my own!

15

My Treasure Saved Me

In the spring of 1950 before Georges stopped working, my friend Paul was offered a promotion far away. He was willing to decline it to stay with me. I encouraged him very much to accept and not ruin his career on my account. Inwardly, I knew divorce was not the answer, and we could not continue our secret relationship indefinitely. We talked about it, and he asked if "*I*" wanted him to marry me. "What? You ask me if *I* want? Had you said that *you* wanted to marry me, that would have been totally different." I shook my head and said "no." His approach showed me his weakness and cut short our relationship.

No, I did not want another weak man. I needed someone strong, determined, who could make decisions and lead me in life. I never met such a man, *until*...well, until I met the Lord.

I had told Paul, a Princeton graduate, that I always believed in God up in heaven, but how about Jesus Christ? Who is He? He had answered that there were many ways to God, and that Christ was just one of the ways. After painfully searching for four years, I found out that it was not so. The Word says, "*Christ is the door, the only way, the truth and the life.*"

My husband was needling me at every opportunity, always against my business. While he was working and occupied, Georges would come home, eat, listen to the radio and retire early. He was leading his life, leaving me to lead mine. However, having stopped working, he had too much time on his hands and spent a lot of it finding fault with me. He became intensely jealous of my success, and that jealousy made him irrational and blind, biting the hand that fed him. Of course his male ego was frustrated, and he took it out on me.

My nerves were becoming frayed. I had to rest much that summer. Fortunately I could count on my two salesgirls, one in town and the other at the lake, to carry on the business.

There was a need to go on a buying trip to New York. I saw Georgette, who invited me for a few days to Lake Placid in the Adirondacks. The room overlooked the lake. An overwhelming sense of a presence woke me in the night. I went to the window. There was a shimmering silver reflection of the full moon on the dark lake. The evergreen trees and the hills were silhouetted in black against the starry sky. The landscape seemed palpitating with life. I became God-conscious. God! God is the one I needed. I had to find Him. But where and how? For the time being, I kept my secret. There was no one to share it with.

Back in Kalamazoo, while reflecting in bed upon how I would manage three stores, I was stopped in my consideration. The inner voice returned and intervened, "You are successful in your business. You will have a chain reaction from coast to coast. This will take all your time. You will be married to your business and there will be no time to find answers to life."

Answers to life! I was astonished. There are answers to life! My life was getting more and more muddled. I needed to find the answers. I was eager to pay the price no matter what. God must have something to do with the answers, I thought. I must find God above all else. Forget the third store.

Labor Day was approaching. After the weekend, the tourist trade in Saugatuck would stop, and I decided to close this second store.

Georges knew nothing of my plans. He was uncooperative, jealous of my success. He had been threatening for months to cut up my face with a butcher knife. His moments of rage came closer and closer together. Every evening he listened to one murder mystery after another on the radio. What morbid taste, I thought.

One evening, as we argued, I said, "Why don't you just go away? Why don't you leave me? The earth is simply not big enough to hold people of such opposite views. Your behavior makes me think that you want to get rid of me. I handed him his shotgun. "Come on, shoot me if you have the nerve."

He didn't take the gun; instead he said, "I am going to take the car and kill myself."

"Okay, go. I'll see you later because you do not have the courage to kill yourself either. You love yourself and the car too much." He returned a couple of hours later and drove the car in the garage. I heard the garage door slam. Looking out the window, I realized the car was still running and Georges was inside. Was he really trying to kill himself with the carbon monoxide, or just pretending? It was after midnight. I was not going to interfere, but I did call the only friend he cultivated, a psychiatrist. The state hospital where the doctor lived and worked was very close; he came in a matter of minutes. He called Georges to come out of the garage and asked him to wait outside while he talked with me.

"Why did you call me?" was his question.

"I could not in cold blood let a man kill himself. You are his friend; so I called."

"What is going on?"

"We are two absolute opposites. We are growing further and further apart. There is no common ground; we have no common friends, no common interests. I am very busy, while he has time to make my life unbearable. Why does he not leave?" He listened attentively and then called Georges, but asked me to stay.

"Georges, you are the loser," said the doctor and left. I went to my bedroom and slept. I saw that Georges was building a case against me. Was he getting ideas from the murder mysteries he was hearing on the radio, I wondered? Did that explained his constant provocations the past year, trying to prove me insane? Was his friendship with the psychiatrist for this purpose? If so, it did not work. Thank God, the doctor saw through something.

I knew I had to sell the store and leave. My nerves could take no more. In addition, it so happened that I found a drawer under the kitchen table that I had not seen before. All it contained were three small envelopes from a pharmacy, each identified: cyanide, arsenic, copper oxide. They certainly were not intended for rats, for there were none in our clean residential neighborhood. I calmly removed them and threw them in the garbage can. Today I would certainly have done it differently. But then I simply did not let on. Let Georges wonder, I thought.

I was so inexperienced. I did not know how to defend myself nor how to get help. I did not even know that I could get help. One thing I knew was that my life was at stake.

I needed to go to Chicago for some more merchandise, and as I entered the train station, my ever present inner Voice spoke loud and clear, "Go, you are free." My mind went into high gear. By the time I reached the ticket counter, I ordered a ticket for the following night: "One way. New York City, please."

In the evening I told Georges that I was leaving for New York the following night. "I know," he said, "because I hired a detective to follow you. I need a check for $75 to pay him." I did not even respond. I wrote out the check. It was cheaper than to argue.

Noblesse oblige.

The next morning I was advised that Georges' lawyer was coming to have me sign a financial agreement. It was to be so simple! We'll divide our assets in half. I would keep the store (remember that Georges never had anything to do with it). It was mine anyway. He would keep the house and the car. How about my share? I did not say a word and went to my bedroom to pick up my handbag, a night gown, and a tooth brush, and left the house disgusted. The worst was yet to come.

There was time to stop at a realtor and put my store up for sale. The sales girl was willing to keep it open. I asked for the price of the inventory, ten thousand dollars wholesale. But Georges told the realtor later that it was not worth that much. The realtor, without checking it out, put a price of six thousand dollars and found a serious buyer within a week. I had to come back from New York to take the inventory with the buyer and close the sale. I still did not know the price had been cut.

I spent the night in a hotel. At breakfast I inadvertently sat opposite a number of businessmen, each at his own little table, all facing the same direction, all reading the morning paper, all wearing a gray suit and a red tie, all cut out of the same mold: the business establishment. I laughed inwardly. What a bore. I did not know yet where I belonged, but *this* was not my world either.

After finishing the inventory, I was not only faced with this poor offer but with the fact that Georges had attached the store to pay off his debts of four thousand dollars. I knew nothing about such a raw deal.

However, life is more precious than money. I came out of an ordeal with my life, with two thousand dollars in cash, and had escaped a nest of vipers. With an exhilarating sense of relief, I boarded the train. The drum beat of the wheels on the rails echoed a song of deliverance and victory in my heart. I was free!

A couple of weeks later someone in New York asked if I were not from Kalamazoo. "Yes, I am."

"A man killed his wife there last week," he said.

"Oh," I replied, "that bullet was meant for me." The evil power over Georges had found another target. My Treasure had saved my life!

16

Greenwich Village

The Search

In a few days I had an apartment in Greenwich Village, a five-floor walk-up. I liked that. It gave me protection, just in case Georges came looking for me. Sure enough, the concierge told me that a man from Kalamazoo came to see me, but he could not handle the stairs and left. I was saved again!

The old streets of Greenwich Village had a particularly bad smell from the dead skin cells shed by previous generations. After a while you became accustomed to it. A Russian acquaintance came to paint the entire place, and I had the hall and living room carpeted in shades of fawn. Somehow the sewing machine was forwarded to me, and I made the draperies, almond green for the living room and turquoise for the bedroom. I took an afternoon to buy the furniture, and within a week I was at home, really at home and settled. I could relax.

The physical efforts of the past weeks were almost superhuman. My nerves, already frayed, were stretched to the breaking point. I definitely experienced a nervous breakdown. I lost sense of direction and of time—seconds seemed too long. I was terribly frightened to go underground to take the subway and traveled on foot or by bus. Most people looked like demons. I had become clairvoyant. To shield myself, I would stay home three days at a time, resting, taking two hot baths a day, listening to classical music on the radio to soothe my nerves and burning twelve-inch logs in my toy but real fireplace. For an even more relaxing environment I would use candles instead of the electric light.

Following what I then called my hunches, I knew what to do. There was only one part of me that was sick; the other part, deep within, was guiding me when I turned to it. Some people call it instinct. Did I need to see a psychiatrist? No! I only needed to listen to my inner self.

I cooked very simple meals, avoiding sugars and fats. At the Italian vegetable and fruit stand, an elderly little Jewish man started to talk to me. "Are you a vegetarian?"

"No."

"You can get uric poisoning from eating too much meat." He talked on and on. It made sense. I should try vegetarianism. Since he lived in the neighborhood, I saw him again, and he introduced me to the two juice bars and the one health food store in Manhattan in 1951. That was all there was! There also was a little bookroom on a second floor that carried a handful of books on natural health and some magazines. One book was on "Toxicity: The Base of Disease." I bought it and it opened my eyes. I had to be detoxified. Fruits, vegetables, raw juices, and cereals would do it. Little by little I eased off meat. In the past I had been eating meat three times a day. Occasionally the craving for it was very intense, but I was determined to stick with my new diet. By the end of the year my diet was one hundred percent vegetarian. I also learned to fast and I fasted regularly on Saturdays, with great delight. It made me feel so very peaceful as the body could rest from the intense activities of digestion.

My nerves were healing. I was no longer clairvoyant nor afraid of the underground as my fears subsided some. I became friendly with people and no longer crouched in the back of the bus, but came forward to talk to the driver. Once, boarding the bus on 59th Street and 6th Avenue to return to the village, I greeted the driver and asked him how he was on such a beautiful afternoon. "Lady," he said, putting his hand over the coin machine, "this ride is on me. You made my day. You are the first one to greet me since I took this shift in the morning. Where are you going?"

"Home to the Village."

"Have you ever been to the Bowery? No? Then you can ride with me to the end of the line to see the Statue of Liberty and then back home." It seems like my simple greeting was not much, yet it touched his feelings and he responded with kindness. I still remember it, and I am sure that he too remembered it for a long time. It taught me to care for people and to be kind and considerate toward them.

There was another heartwarming occasion. As I was coming home one evening all dressed up, after a matinee at the theater, a whiff of roasted chestnuts from a street vendor reminded me of Paris. "It smells like Paris," I told the vendor. He handed me a cornet and added two more chestnuts. As I was taking off my white kid gloves and opening my purse, he said, "Take it. This is a gift." I was so surprised, and I hesitated to take the living from a poor vendor, but then I considered it a blessing for both of us, a blessing to the giver and to the receiver.

There was a time when I never would have stooped to talk to a street vendor, a bus driver, or a little man at the market. Today I recognize them as God walking on earth, healing people. These heartwarming situations helped a great deal. I was well enough to start working, but still far from being completely healed.

Altmans hired me as a sales lady for their coat department. After a couple of months our personnel manager called me to her office. "Business is very slow," she said. "I am sorry to have to lay you off as you were the last one hired, but before you go, stop by the general office to say hello to the girls. They want to see what someone with such a high I.Q. looks like." I was not told nor did I ask what the I.Q. was, but I remember that test. I was on such a nervous high that I raced through the questions full speed, skipping over a few that presented any hesitation. I came home to my quiet nest.

Nothing made any sense. Why would they fire me if they valued my I.Q.? Nothing really mattered. Why was I on this earth anyway? No one consulted me. I was put here and had to pay rent. Why am I here and what more is there to do? I had seen enough—the scenery was only repeating itself. I had heard enough—music can only satisfy so much. I had tasted enough—you can eat only so much food. I had touched and smelled, and self-gratification ran out. The sense of futility and the vanity of it all overcame me. There was nothing left for me to do. All was vanity. I was empty. Why live? I had come to the end of myself at the age of thirty-five.

As I seriously considered turning on the gas at night and going to sleep, never to wake up again, I found that it was not so simple. My inner Voice kept bothering me: "Then what?" I realized that indeed I could kill my body, but how about my soul, my self? I had no power nor a way to kill my inner self. Suddenly everything changed. I felt that I was at the gate of Paradise, at the threshold of light. Yes, there was something more to live for. I fell into a deep, relaxing sleep.

Positive Thinking

I woke up refreshed and went about my household activities, considering what to do next. I remembered that Mr. Klein, a friend of Georgette, had a custom rug company on Madison Avenue. He received me very kindly: indeed, I could do the public relations work for him since he had no time for it. It was a dream of a job. I came into contact with a very positive and optimistic crowd and went on the positive thinking bandwagon—but not the religious positive thinking of Norman Vincent Peale.

Dressed like a model with my rug samples in a hat box—the model's trademark—I contacted every well-known interior designer and some architects in New York. I had a happy, smiling and positive approach. Every door was open without appointments. I worked well and lost no time. Within three to four months the rounds were made, and I turned over my file of 3-by-5 cards, one for every visit and prospective client. Now it was up to the salesman to sell our product. Our best seller cost ninety dollars a yard!

"What will you do next?" asked my boss.

"I do not know."

"How about spending a couple of months in Puerto Rico with the factory where the rugs are hand-looped? We have apartments next door for the designers and a swimming pool. After learning the process of custom rug making and marketing, I'll give you a sales territory."

"For that I'll need a car."

"We'll give you a car."

"I don't know how to drive."

"We'll give you a chauffeur."

"Where will the territory be?"

"New England, Boston."

"The New Englanders are very sober, straight-laced, steeped in customs and traditions. I won't fit in." While this conversation was going on, I knew inwardly that I could not accept such a responsibility. I would have to tie myself down for ten years. This is not what I wanted to do the rest of my life. What about finding God?

"Sorry, Sir. I cannot take on the job."

"What will you do?"

"I do not know."

It sounded absolutely irrational. Outwardly, my reactions were senseless. There was no logic, not even a sense of self-preservation. All I had was a strong, inner feeling of righteous behavior toward Mr. Klein. I could not just take advantage of a vacation in Puerto Rico and leave.

There was one more business possibility I wanted to explore before leaving New York. The thought of leaving had come to me during my last visit to Interior Designers at the Rockefeller Center. Looking out the windows of a plush penthouse in the Center, I could see nothing but gray masses down below, masses of gray cement buildings cut up by crevasses of streets. People were there crawling like ants, every one rushing somewhere in opposite directions. The question arose, "What am I doing here in New York?"

However, to prove my positive approach theory, I needed to contact one more person. Through my business contacts I came to hear about a man who was called King of the Pearl because he acquired most of the natural pearl fields of ocean beds. He was a Russian Jew, red-headed and ruddy like King David. He had to flee from his apartment on the Champs Elysées in Paris during the war, just ahead of the Nazis. He was living in a sumptuous Fifth Avenue hotel which rivaled the Waldorf Astoria in elegance.

Here was indeed a wonderful opportunity to exercise my positive thinking. I had come to sell myself. My public relations experience, my modeling ability, my languages, and general culture all could serve to sell the natural pearl to the jewelers and the socialites of New York. I had the job ninety-nine percent in my pocket since the gentleman was supportive of me. "Yes, you could be the right person for the job. *But...*"

There was an element I had not counted on. The Japanese had killed the natural pearl market by introducing the cultured pearl. Its public reception was excellent, and the price was unbeatable. The King of the Pearl was checkmated! And so was I. I could not land the last one percent. By the time we were ready to go, there was no market. Therefore, positive thinking is not everything. I stopped in my tracks and threw positive thinking overboard. There must be something else to consider, that is, the will of God. The French say, "*Man proposes but God disposes.*"

Yoga?

I had considered so many avenues of thought already. I read excerpts of one philosopher after another, excerpts of the Koran and the Kabalah, attended courses on comparative religion at New York University, all the time seeking. Where was God?

The Hindus had the answer, I was told. Study and practice the different yogas, and find yourself a guru. He'll teach you meditation. Then you can travel to the Himalayas and be perfected. I did not have that kind of money, but I could find a guru teacher. I found a woman guru, a Russian who had been in the Himalayas ten years. Good enough. But had she met God? No! "God is not a person," she said. "Nirvana is the greatest thing, the creative power in the universe. You must sit cross legged, empty your mind, and merge into nothingness." Well, I would try anything. And I started my yoga lessons once a week. I *had* to find God.

However, I met a seeking lady, and I decided to also check out the prestigious Theosophical Society. We went to an open meeting. The atmosphere was very solemn and dark. Mostly men were present; I felt a little embarrassed. The gist of their philosophy was that no one had come to God because God dwells in unapproachable light surrounded by a veil. All religions are on the same quest of the Holy Grail, all are stopped by this impenetrable veil, and all are endeavoring to pierce through. We went to some powerful lectures by renowned philosophers, like A. Huxley, and joined the society. But we would come out of a meeting even more perplexed, wondering how do we pierce through the veil, and where do we go next? One afternoon, as Nadia and I were taking a walk on Fifth Avenue, we stopped at the construction site of the Guggenheim Museum. We both recognized the architect, Frank Lloyd Wright, having heard him lecture. He came to us as we stood at the fence. We voiced our appreciation for his work. He asked me what my life work was. "I do not know. I have not found it yet." Yes! What was I supposed to be? I did well as a kindergarten teacher, well as a dress designer and maker, well as a business woman, and well in public relations. I was changing professions every two years. By applying myself and studying I could succeed in just about everything outside of ballet and opera! The futility of life had struck me the year before when I considered suicide. One thing I had not succeeded at was finding God and my purpose in life.

How did life start? How did this whole universe start? The 42nd Street Library was a forty-minute walk from my apartment. I often went there on my days off, going up the steps between the two lions sitting there as sphinxes, guarding the unsolved mysteries on the bookshelves—mysteries I tried to penetrate. Little did I know that all the answers were contained in one little book called the Bible.

So I kept searching. I wanted to discover the beginning of things, the origin of continents, risen or sunken, the origin of peoples, languages, hieroglyphics, alphabets, religions, etc. I had already come to the conclusion that traditions, conventions, habits, and cultures were meaningless, changing from country to country or changing at the whim of any event.

I realized that I wanted something eternal, and the need in me was clamoring. On the wall above my couch I wanted to write *Amour, Eternité!* I could not recognize that such desire was the prompting of God within me! I was so very dense in my spiritual understanding. I might have had a high I.Q. and a versatility of natural aptitudes, but I was ignorant and stupid when it came to spiritual comprehension. Therefore, I kept on searching outwardly, not realizing that the answer was in me—the Treasure that had guided me all my life was God!

The question arose again, "What was I doing in New York?" I inquired of the U.S. Chamber of Commerce in Washington, D.C., as to where the best climate was, and they informed me that Alpine, California, was the best, where the hot desert air blended with the cool ocean breeze. Delightful! Being close to New York University there was no problem subletting my apartment to students during the school terms. This allowed me to spend the winter in California and the summer in town. A sense of freedom and hope encouraged me.

"*He has made every thing beautiful in its time; He also has planted eternity in men's heart and mind (a divinely implanted sense of a purpose working through the ages which nothing under the sun, but only God, can satisfy...)*" Ecclesiastes 3:11, from the The Amplified Bible.

17

Alpine

The End of the Search

Off I went on the bus, from one coast to the other, stopping in major cities to visit the library, asking about God, then going on the next bus. And so I went for three and a half years to and from the Atlantic to the Pacific talking about God without ever meeting anyone who could give me a realistic answer. I was not interested in heaven. Heaven could take care of itself. I wanted answers that would work in my life, right here, right now. I wanted that kind of a personal God.

Alpine was the home of rugged individualists, thinkers, writers, searchers who had come there to be away from it all. It was easy to strike up a conversation at the library, at the post office, at the grocery store.

I spent the first winter there in a trailer reading an incredible mixture of books. Their intent was to mix you up even more. I was really mixed up and disorganized in thought until I had a supernatural experience. I audibly heard my name called at night, "Helena." It was a deep, compelling voice. Thinking it was my invisible guru, I replied that I was not ready yet. Ready for what? I did not know—ready to follow, I guess.

I had another experience at night. Suddenly I found myself looking down at my body from the ceiling. My psyche had left my body! This was great, I thought. I could visit people anywhere, any time. Such extravaganza was promptly ended with the charge, "Go back. The time is not yet." Don't ask me to explain, for I cannot. But I learned how dangerous disembodiment can be. Some had told me that our psyche is connected to our body by an invisible thread. They told me that if it breaks, you have no way back and remain a disembodied spirit in Satan's realm. Another evil spirit will occupy your body. No thanks!

What I experienced in these quiet and serene surroundings was a newly found oneness with nature. Rabbits, squirrels, and birds became so tame. The body odor of a vegetarian, unlike that of a meat eater, does not frighten the little animals. Their instinct is very acute. They would come around for company's sake. One little bird in particular came to my olive grove over and over again, "telling" me his troubles with the other birds. He just had to complain to someone. Once I put out my hand, and he came to sit on it. I was so thrilled to deserve such trust.

Summer came. Back in New York I quickly got a sales job in one of the many dress shops on Fifth Avenue. I resumed yoga. The physical exercises were particularly beneficial. I also resumed the Washington Square gatherings after work, discussing God with my bench philosophers.

One day as we were talking about New York news, I was told that Lippizaner Horses with their riders were coming to Madison Square Garden from Vienna. I had seen them in their stables in Vienna. Now I had to go, to see them perform. What an unforgettable and thrilling performance that was. Against the velvety black of the unlit arena, the intense spotlights remained focused on the riders and the white horses performing with such grace and agility—it was a dazzling show in the light.

The Village had a weekly paper, very unique. Occasionally I would pick one up. This time it was encouraging us to attend a dinner given for the mayor of New York by the Villagers. The cover charge was six dollars. If I could pay six dollars to see horses at Madison Square Garden, I certainly would pay six dollars to meet the mayor. I designed a special dress for the occasion and came a little late. "Are you alone, Madame?" asked the maitre D'.

"Yes, I am."

"I have just the table for you."

I was seated between two Custom Court judges, at the judges' table! Judge Lawrence sat at my right. We became acquainted. He invited me to visit his office, which I did. Once he asked me to accompany him to some boring dinner party. "My wife is an invalid and cannot come. I'll speak favorably of you to my wife, because some of the other women *they* might choose as escorts for me are more than I can take." *They* referred to the big export-importers who expected to influence the judge by wining and dining him, hoping to buy his favor, thus to pay a lesser duty. No money could buy this New Englander. We both laughed. At least the food was good.

At the next invitation, we decided, we would have *them* take us to the 21 Club. We would go as people watchers. Judge Lawrence was quite an elderly man, appointed as a senior Custom Court judge in the 'thirties by Franklin D. Roosevelt. There must have been a strong reason for a Democratic president to appoint a Republican. If power is determined by the amount of money one controls, then the judge was second to the president. Export-import is a big business. Judge Lawrence was impeccable.

"Would you like to be introduced to President Eisenhower?" he asked me once. I was very surprised and somewhat taken aback.

"Well..., I have nothing to say, nothing to offer." Actually I had plenty to say about the United States trusting the Communists after the war, about giving half of Europe to them, about taking General Patton out of Czechoslovakia, and more. But I was not completely over my nervous breakdown and at times I would become confused and could not organize my thoughts well enough to speak them clearly. I had to cover up the holes in my cognitive function to keep people from realizing that on occasion I was swimming.

"Well," he said, "I'll make you an honorary judge." The judge gave me a gown to put on and a gavel. I sat down on the judge's bench. He told me to call the court to order! I used my gavel and called, "*the court come to order.*" The hall was empty.

"I hereby appoint you honorary judge," he said. We were playing like children—it was so refreshing!

Sometimes, life is like a game, a theater where we act out different roles. By then, I felt I had lived thirty-seven lives, one for each one of my years.

I kept on exploring, putting different powers and religions to the test. I looked into metaphysics, into psychic powers, into occultism and spiritualism. They gave me cold goose bumps. Some promoted the survival of the fittest, but survival for what? Nothing met the demands of my built-in standard, the Treasure that kept guiding me.

For the third time, I went back to my writer's cabin in California that I had rented the winter before, in order to pursue my search for God amidst the hills, the mountain lilac and scrub oak.

The little garden around the cabin was terraced, and I grew radishes, green leaf lettuce, and spinach, all fast-growing things that sprout even in the California winter. I was taking in one hundred ten dollars a month from my renters in the Village, which left me sixty dollars after paying my landlord there. The rent on the cabin was twenty-five dollars, and the thirty-five left was sufficient to supply my vegetarian diet. I had no other needs.

My diet consisted of fruits and nuts in the morning, of a mostly raw vegetable salad for lunch, and a cooked meal of a variety of cereals and beans for supper. Everything was delicious and healthy. I tried to pay attention to the natural rhythm of my body which set a pattern for my days. Bedtime was with the chickens. I awoke at three o'clock in the morning refreshed, ready to work, to read, to think, to write, while munching on fruit and nuts. I had an hour-long yoga physical exercise and meditation. Around eleven I was ready for the kitchen, to fix a scrumptious, big salad. By noon I would take a shower with water warmed by the sun, followed by an hour's nap. This schedule gave me another five-hour workday. My physical work consisted of gardening, clearing patches of land, terracing and taking a two-hour walk to the village and back. My evening meal was cooked. I was happy with myself and thought that I was doing great. I expected to find God through yoga.

Let There be Light

Then I had a tremendous experience. While sitting yoga fashion in meditation trying to empty my mind, words appeared: *And God said, Let there be light and there was light!* I jumped up, saying aloud, "The greatest thing is not nothingness; the greatest thing is the spoken word of God. God spoke the creation into being." Goodbye Nirvana. I burned the yoga books on the spot, and when my California yoga teacher came I made this stupendous declaration about the power of the Word of God, and about burning the books. The man turned livid and walked off, angry.

Soon after, I had a dreadful experience. I could see myself at the very tip of a long branch over a precipice with no way to go on. I had eliminated all traditions, conventions, and culture. Neither philosophy nor religion were the answers. I had just about eliminated man. Now what! It was a short but terrifying trance.

I resumed my daily routine and continued my writing. I was elaborating on what could constitute a perfect human society. If ants have an ant society and bees have a bee society that works perfectly for them, why does not man have one? There also needed to be a book standing against the philosophies of Engels and Marx (communism was based on their writings), and against Hitler. After much consideration, I concluded that a perfect society had to be patterned after a most perfect plan or structure, but it could not be only three-dimensional, nor static. Therefore it had to be an organism, something living. I kept rambling on in my thoughts. The most perfect organism being man, the society had to be patterned after the human body.

I became very excited. This analogy had already begun. We speak of the *head* of the government! I was interrupted by a knock at the door. What a pleasant surprise! These two Alpine villagers were my first visitors. They were also seekers and came to tell me that they were sent by the Spirit of God and that I should obtain a Bible. My reaction was, "That old book?" I quickly apologized for such a disparaging remark.

"Forgive me. I have learned to be objective and not to judge something I know nothing about. Yes, I will obtain a Bible. Thank you."

The Culmination

They left. I went on my walk and stopped at a neighbor's asking where I could find a Bible. She had an extra one and gladly gave it to me. Back home I put it on the shelf and resumed my own thoughts and analogies of a society patterned after the human body. Indeed, we already have the expressions: the legislative *body*, the *members* of Congress, the *organs* of government! Wow! This analogy only needed to be developed further. The system of communication was to be the nervous system. But what about the demand and supply of every member of society, which is our greatest need and shortcoming? What would be the corresponding analogy? My answer was the *blood*. The blood carries the nourishment to every cell, supplies it, satisfies it, and carries away the debris. There had to be a branch of government fulfilling that function. I suddenly felt very sober and rose up for something only to find myself prostrate on the floor under a mighty power.

It was the power of the Almighty. I did not dare think, nor speak, nor even breathe. Then there was a slow and awesome inward speaking, "Don't you think that I have thought of it? [referring to my society] I do not need you. The Kingdom of God is the answer. You are headed for outer darkness."

I could visualize myself disintegrating into black nothingness. Then I saw myself crawling as a worm with my head lifted up high in pride.

"If you were to come back to life, what would you want to be—a movie star?"

"No." I felt offended. "I would like to warn seven or eight other women not to go my way."

Now I sensed the presence of a spiritual body standing at my right. I did not know who it was. The Almighty voice said, "What you are looking for is in Jesus. He is the Man. He is the prototype of the human society I have established." A veil lifted, and inwardly I saw, and I understood. Jesus was the prototype of a perfect divine society, and it was all in the Book, all written in the Bible. He was the one standing at my side, and He had been the Voice in me through all my years. Now, this day, *it pleased the Father to reveal His Son in me.*

I was still laying motionless on the cold floor when warm blood started flowing within me, to my extremities, making me realize that I had been laying there as cold as death, and now the blood was stirring in my veins. The power of the Almighty lifted, and I felt free to breathe, to move, to rise up. In a sense I was devastated, but not annihilated. I was shaken, subdued, to some extent frightened. However this fright was more like reverence. I also saw myself and my pride and repented in tears. Then there was a sense of a comforting Presence. I was not alone, no longer afraid. I picked up the Bible.

Amazing grace, how sweet the sound,
That saved a wretch like me!
I once was lost, but now am found,
Was blind, but now I see.

Part II

18

Slain to Live

Slain under the power of God! You might say that you have not had such an experience; few people have. You probably did not need such drastic treatment. The Lord had other ways to bring you to Himself, and you responded. However, I did not respond in spite of His loving and constant guidance. I did not recognize the gentle speaking and prompting as coming from the Lord. Even when the speaking was strong, there was no awareness on my part that it came from God. I was so dull, stubborn, silly, and closed to God. In my pride, vanity, and presumption I gave myself and my subconsciousness the credit for making the right decisions, and I gave my clever mind the credit for trying to discover a perfect society. But when, in my consideration and writing on the perfect human society, I touched upon the *blood*, I had come to holy ground. "Life and death are in the blood."

In His infinite mercy, God had stopped me. I was on dangerous ground. The only life God recognizes is the eternal life, the life of God; the only blood He recognizes is the *blood* of Christ. I was trespassing and had fallen as if dead. I should have remained dead, but by His infinite mercy, the Father forgave my trespasses and took pleasure in revealing His Son, Jesus, in me.

Jesus! He was my lifelong Treasure sown into my heart as a seed by my grandfather! Grandfather passed away when I was barely three, and no one continued speaking the name of Jesus to me in such an intimate way. I forgot His name, but He did not forget me! He kept on speaking, and the seed kept on growing at those times when I obeyed my inner Voice.

He, Jesus, was the Treasure whom I had not recognized. He was the searching and sweeping Spirit constraining me to seek God then and now, convincing me that I had not found God in my four years of trying, but that God had found me, because He had chosen me in Him before the foundation of the world. Yes, He knew me from my mother's womb.

I had not been able to find Him because I was searching in the wrong realm, in the realm of my mind—searching outwardly while He was speaking to me in my heart. He had already made His home in a little corner of my heart back in my childhood. No wonder I had such a miraculous life; I was rich in my poverty! I was traveling on a hidden miracle lane! Often I thought I was resorting to my own instincts and hunches during difficult times, when actually it was my Treasure within leading me

As I picked up the Bible, I was puzzled. I had never opened this book before. In the Catholic countries of my youth it was a forbidden book, in some places even under the threat of excommunication. We children knew nothing about it; no one mentioned it until I grew up. What did this book contain? The time had come for me to see.

As I sat down and opened the Bible, I found my hands and eyes being directed to a certain page and verse by an irresistible power. I started reading for the very first time from Hebrews 12:22, "*Ye are come unto mount Zion, and unto the city of the living God, the heavenly Jerusalem, and to an innumerable company of angels.*" I read on in amazement verse 23: "*To the general assembly and church of the firstborn, which are written in heaven, and to God the Judge of all, and to the spirits of just men made perfect.*" I was overwhelmed and could not go on. This was all so real, so holy, so full of wonder. I needed time to consider it and let the words sink in. I knew that I had been judged by God, and I sensed the presence of angels in the room. But now I would need to find the "church of the firstborn" and the "just men made perfect." Where were they? These were all heavenly people and I was in my body on earth, yet the Word said I had come. I did not try to explain this revelation, but I knew it was real.

Again my hands were guided to another page and verse, to First Peter 2:2,3,9: "*As newborn babes, desire the sincere milk of the word, that ye may grow thereby: if so be ye have tasted that the Lord is gracious*" and, "*But ye are a chosen generation, a royal priesthood, a holy nation, a peculiar people,...ye are a chosen generation....*" I knew there was something special about me.... "*...a royal priesthood...*" This was the kind of royalty and nobility I was looking for! "*...ye... are a holy nation, a peculiar people.*" No wonder no government on earth satisfied me. My Treasure did not approve of any of those governments. God had His own nation with a kingly people, and this is what I was searching for in my teens and why I was rejecting every government for not coming up to the standard of my heart. Now I had the answer: the Kingdom of God was the perfect society for man. I needed to look no further.

Every word of First Peter 2 was just for me. It was like listening to a living person with whom I was having a conversation. The words were penetrating the depths of my being. I was part of God's people and of His Kingdom. Blood was rushing to my head from sheer excitement. I did not understand it all with my mind, but deep within I knew. The words were overpowering; I had to stop and quiet down.

Again I was led to continue my reading, this time from Matthew chapters five to twelve. Blessed... blessed...blessed... I wrote the blessings out to keep reminding myself that these were the new laws of the kingdom. This was how I should live. Every one of the blessings was so lovable, although in exact opposition to my natural being. I had to keep reading them as a constant reminder (Matt. 5:3-12):

Blessed are the poor in spirit:
for theirs is the kingdom of heaven.
Blessed are they that mourn:
for they shall be comforted.
Blessed are the meek:
for they shall inherit the earth.
Blessed are they which do hunger
and thirst after righteousness:
for they shall be filled.
Blessed are the merciful:
for they shall obtain mercy.
Blessed are the pure in heart:
for they shall see God.
Blessed are the peacemakers:
for they shall be called the children of God.
Blessed are they which are persecuted
for righteousness' sake:
for theirs is the kingdom of heaven.
Blessed are ye, when men shall revile you and persecute you,
and shall say all manner of evil against you falsely,
for my sake. Rejoice, and be exceeding glad:
for great is your reward in heaven:
for so persecuted they the prophets
which were before you.

Angels and Demons

These nine blessings deeply impressed me, showing me how I should live. I had to make a one hundred eighty degree turn to live another way. How could I do that? Well, I received help from within. When asserting myself, to have my own way, there would be a silent reminder of a blessing: "*The meek shall inherit the earth.*" As I was repeating these words there was such a clean feeling. Much later, I discovered what was happening. I was being washed by the water in the Word, and I was drinking the milk that made me grow.

Later that same day, in the kitchen, I tried to pray according to the concepts of religion where you read or recite a pre-composed prayer. The only verses I knew, even in part, were from the Lord's prayer, having heard Gladys Swarthout singing it over the radio during the war years on Sundays. Haltingly, trying to remember the words, I began: "*Our Father who art in heaven...hallowed be...Thy name. Thy kingdom come. Thy will be done....*" I hesitated. In the background I could hear Satan laughing: "You don't know how to pray!" He flustered me. He seemed to be in the kitchen with me. I walked away, trying to recollect the words through the melody. "*Thy will be done on earth as it is in heaven.*" I began to gain confidence. Slowly, word by word, I went on. "*Give me this day my daily bread and forgive me my offenses as I forgive those who offend me. And lead me not into temptation but deliver me from evil.*" I felt relieved and remembered the end very well: "*For Thine is the kingdom and the power and the glory for ever. Amen!*"

Night fell. My stomach had been quiet all day, and now it began to clamor for food. In the kitchen I became confused, sensing the derisory presence of Satan. It made me burn some food. "You see, you even act like a devil, and you look like one," he whispered. I was wearing my jodhpurs and riding boots from my New York days when I would go horseback riding in Central Park. Those clothes now represented something that I enjoyed of the world, and I quickly changed them and regained my peace. After eating, I went to bed, exhausted.

On awakening I grabbed the Bible to refresh my memories of the day before. The following two days I was fluctuating between light and darkness, between the angels and demons. One time, sensing a strong presence which made me uneasy, I asked audibly, "Who are you?"

"We are the White Brotherhood. We will teach you the secrets of the unseen."

"No, thank you. I do not want any intermediary. I want the Holy Spirit to teach me." The (invisible) White Brotherhood left, never to return. Amazingly, I had read in John shortly before that the Comforter, the Holy Spirit, would come and teach me all things. That was divine timing.

Throughout all of my searching years I had read about such things as the White Brotherhood, and I had participated in yoga, thus touching the realm of Satan. I now realized this was a powerful and dangerous realm that should not be touched. At this very moment, having read about the Holy Spirit, I had the highest power to overcome the darkness of these other spirits.

These three days of intense spiritual activities kept me busy, while the heavy and relentless rains of the spring equinox of 1954 were soaking the ground, keeping everyone indoors. A visitor knocked at my door the day after the rains ended, an acquaintance, a lady from New York, who had also come to relax in the wild and to meditate. Here she was with her dachshund asking me to care for the dog for a week during her absence. I did not like "dachsies," but how could I turn her down and make her unhappy? On the other hand, having been convicted of sin, and having felt unworthy of the slightest responsibility, I was flattered to be entrusted with something living, even if it were only a dog.

This little "dachsie" turned out to be my helper. When invisible evil powers came around to attack me, that dog's hair would bristle. He would growl and stare into space, thus alerting me to pick up my Bible and read the Word. This would bring me into the light, and the dark angels would flee. When angels came from God to minister to me, that little doggie would be so happy and would wag his tail. Why? Because he was clairvoyant, and even he disliked the demons and liked the angels. I came to like him in spite of his outer looks and was sad to give him up.

Cleaning House

With such a drastic change of life and vision, all my previous mental activities stopped. They were gone, replaced by the Bible. I read avidly. New avenues of thought, discipline, and behavior were opening up to me. As I continued with the book of Matthew, one verse spoke to me and convicted me. Chapter five, verse 44 says, "*I say unto you, Love your enemies, bless them that curse you, do good to them that hate you, and pray for them which despitefully use you, and persecute you.*" I certainly had been hated, despitefully used, and persecuted. Immediately my ex husband came to mind, and I knew I had to write him, asking for forgiveness for my offenses and bad attitudes toward him. I wrote quickly, while the Spirit was fresh within me, and I was empowered to do it. My conscience had to be cleansed. On one side it hurt my pride, but on the other I felt more at ease.

At that time a membership renewal letter came from the Theosophical Society in New York. This was a God-given opportunity to tell them that I had finished my search and had come through the veil, that there was only one way and one door, which was Jesus. He was the door from darkness to light; I had seen the light. He was the only way, the truth, and the life. I had received a new life, the eternal life. Therefore, I respectfully asked to cancel my membership from the Society. A letter arrived by return mail complimenting me on my experience and offering me an honorary membership to the Society, which I had to decline.

Other details bothered my conscience, for example, my wardrobe. I sensed that some clothes were immodest: the shorts, the halters, the sleeveless dresses, and a very masculine-looking gray flannel tailored suit that had been my pride and joy. No one had to tell me. My built-in indicator did some active work, reminding me that there were more books and papers to be burned. I gladly complied.

Then the apartment in New York had to be vacated. I was really cleaning house! Since I had decided not to return, I called a friend from the Washington Square crowd who had written that his wife of ten years had left, leaving him with two children. "Could he please take over my apartment?" I asked. The rent was cheaper, and he could have all my good furniture except for the sewing machine, which was to be sold. I did need a little cash! He agreed. This was the quickest, cleanest, shortest transaction in my life. The family lived in the apartment until his children went to college. God had set the stage to satisfy everyone.

While eating my delicious, vegetarian supper that night, my inner voice asked me to give up my strict diet because at the time this was a radical way of living that other Christians might not understand, making me an outsider. I wanted to be so absolute and obedient to the Lord in whatever He might request of me. Fruits and vegetables were not in the mainstream of American diet as they are today; however, I was not asked to give up my habit of fasting from time to time. I read in Matthew that I should *fast unto the Father*. I loved it. When I needed an answer, help, or understanding, I would fast and invariably obtain results.

My responsibilities were lifted. I had no other burden. Feeling so clean, I was happy, until one day I had a fleeting vision of myself. Sandwiched between two fluffy white clouds was a layer of black soot. There I was, looking so clean and fresh on the outside, yet with so much work to be done by the Lord inwardly.

19

Entering a Walk of Trust

Principles

The thought came: how will I go on with my life? The answers also came as I kept reading on in Matthew, chapter six. "*For where your treasure is, there will your heart be also.*" My Treasure was already heavenly and not material. I had learned that lesson from youth. To me, money was secondary.

"*No man can serve two masters...ye cannot serve God and mammon.*"

"I do not know who mammon is, but, Lord, I want to serve you," was my plea.

"*Therefore I say unto you,*"—the Lord was speaking directly to me through His word— "*Take no thought for your life, what ye shall eat, or what ye shall drink; nor yet for your body, what ye shall put on. Is not the life more than meat and the body than raiment?*" It certainly is; how many times had I escaped death and run for life? I ran from Russia; I ran from the convents; I ran from Czechoslovakia; I ran from my husband. Sometimes I wondered, "Am I a coward?"

No. Instinctively I kept a principle: *choose life!* Now, I could choose divine life. The written words kept on speaking: "*Behold the fowls of the air: for they sow not, neither do they reap, nor gather into barns; yet your heavenly Father feedeth them. Are ye not much better than they?"*

"Lord, I have lived like a sparrow most of my life. You have proved this word to me as I now reflect upon it."

"*And why take ye thought for your raiment? Consider the lilies of the field... Wherefore, if God so clothed the grass of the field which today is and tomorrow is cast into the oven, shall He not much more clothe you? O ye of little faith.*"

"Lord, I want to be a sparrow in Your hand and a lily in Your field. I believe this."

"*But seek ye first the kingdom of God, and His righteousness; and all these things shall be added unto you.*"

I felt so full I could contain no more. Later people would ask me: "Helena, what are you doing?"

I would tell them, "I am seeking the kingdom of God."

"Oh?" they would respond

God tried to govern my life through the principles I had read in Matthew. Often I kept them; more often I failed; however, I learned to take His infinite mercy and go on. He never failed, but He did keep testing me. When asked to give my last dollar to someone who needed it more than I, I gladly complied. It would come back multiplied.

Now, still in my writer's cabin, I was on my last dollar. I finished the little bit of food left in the kitchen and started packing, reducing my possessions to two suitcases that I could carry. It was up to God to give me direction. I only knew that I had to move because there was no provision for the rent. It was April.

I was standing in the middle of the room with the suitcases on either side of me: "Where do I go from here?"

I received an answer: "Walk a straight path with your head in the cloud, your feet firmly planted on the ground, and do whatever comes your way to the right and to the left. Do not try to break down walls nor pound on closed doors. Learn to walk from open heart to open heart and meet the people's need." These words, as well as all that had come to me in the past ten days, were deeply engraved in the depth of my being. I felt secure and confident. God was equipping me for life.

"*In all your ways acknowledge me, and I shall direct your path.*" This was the last comforting speaking received in the cabin.

I looked outside, and lo and behold two ladies were coming to my door. I opened before they had had time to knock. "Welcome ! Welcome! What brings you here?" I asked.

"We are from the Community Church and we have come to ask a favor of you."

"Enter, please." The gist of it was that an elderly missionary needed someone to stay with her in the absence of her husband. Would I be her companion for a month? I told them that I could accept without hesitation because I was waiting for something to happen and my suitcases were already packed. They were amazed! I was thankful.

A missionary! Maybe she could help. Since the Bible began to be opened to me, I read it daily, hours on end. Some of it I read out of curiosity; some of it went over my head. But much of the printed Word spoke to me directly, leaving me in a state of wonder. My conversion was so fresh and so strong that my questions must have overpowered the dear lady.

On Sunday we went to the Community Church. Nothing particularly touched me until the announcement of a baptism ceremony. I wanted to be baptized. "Do you go to a river for that?" I asked innocently.

"No, no, here you are sprinkled."

"I do not want that," I replied. "I want to follow Jesus. He said, 'Follow me,' and He went to a river to be immersed. I want to be immersed also."

"Then you need to go to the Baptists." There were no Baptist churches in Alpine. I had to wait a year.

The ladies of the Community Church invited me for a potluck dinner. I was full of expectation, wanting a rich fellowship in the Word. Instead I encountered nothing but small talk. The name of Jesus was not even mentioned. I was totally disappointed and did not return to their meetings.

I loved to walk and did not mind doing the missionary's shopping for food. On the contrary, it was a blessing. Nature had put on a new garb since my conversion. Everything looked so fresh and sparkling. The skies were bluer, the trees greener, the flowers more radiant, and everything was shimmering, shimmering inside of me also. I went skipping along like a child, thanking God for a newfound happiness, which filled the void in my life. One afternoon on my walk, God spoke: "You must open your mouth and confess my name." I was a little frightened and shared my feeling with the missionary. She pointed me to a verse in Romans 10:10, "*For with the heart man believeth unto righteousness; and with the mouth confession is made unto salvation.*"

"Testify to strangers?" I asked.

She answered, "Yes, to strangers."

Do You Need a Ride?

The opportunity to open my mouth and testify came right away. When I was walking on the road to the village, a car stopped: "Do you need a ride?"

The car was junky and the characters shady, but I was with God. Although I really did not need a ride, I accepted. The men let me have a front seat, and I started speaking immediately: "You know, you had your intentions for giving me a ride, but the Lord Jesus has another. He wants me to tell you about Him." The atmosphere changed. The guys felt uneasy: "Where do you want to get off?" They could not get rid of me fast enough.

"Take me a little further, please, to the village—right here will be all right." I was enjoying the situation without being facetious.

After that episode, I said, "Lord, let's make a deal. You give me the rides, and I will witness to your saving grace." I would follow the missionary's prompting.

"*With the heart man believes unto righteousness, and with the mouth confession is made unto salvation.*" I had just been saved from a situation that could have turned ugly. At another time I was walking along a eucalyptus-lined back road amongst orange groves, enjoying my own Garden of Eden. The vibrant silence of nature was broken by the putt-putt of an old car. It was like a replica of the Beverly Hillbillies. To my surprise, they stopped: "Do you need a ride?"

"Do you really have room?" The kids huddled together, and I got in with my pretty, clean dress. How could I refuse such open hearts. We thanked the Lord in unison.

Another episode transpired about a year later in Colton, California. I was traveling in a car with students from a theological seminary. We were on the way to Palm Springs to give our testimonies. The driver needed half an hour to check out the car and asked us to return on time, or else...

On Main Street I noticed a teenager, looking miserable, and my inner voice said, "Follow her." She turned on a side street and headed for the railroad tracks. She stopped there and bent down to listen to the sound carried by the rails, which probably advised of an oncoming train. I followed fifty feet behind her, and her intentions became evident. My part in the drama was evident also. I could not leave her. I approached her and started talking about the weather, about the town, anything to distract her and open her up.

"Let us sit down on these rail ties and talk." I introduced Jesus into our conversation and spoke of His love for her. He could help in her distress. She told me that she had left home and spent the night with some guys. She was also drunk. After a few minutes she got up and said to my horror, "I feel better. I am going to have another beer!"

"Lord! I cannot leave her now, and I am about to miss my ride." I spotted her going into a beer parlor, and I kept on walking.

"Lord, she is a minor. Should I turn her in to the police? Is that what You would do? NO! What should I do?" I had walked three blocks past the beer parlor when a car stopped:

"Do you need a ride?"

"Yes, sir, do I ever need a ride!" I told him about the girl. She was from Riverside and needed to be driven home. "You are a Godsend!" He agreed to help, but asked me to go inside the parlor, as he did not feel at ease to go in. I had no problem. The girl was sitting at the counter, beer in hand. I took the mug and plunked it on the counter.

"You are coming with me." The woman bartender looked bewildered, and said, referring to the teenager, "She is a nice girl."

"One more reason she should not be here." I picked her up by the collar and led her out. My collaborator was parked in front. We had to push the girl into the back seat, and we no sooner took off than she collapsed into a deep sleep. Where do we go from here? All I knew was that Riverside was her hometown. I told my co-worker about my missing a ride to Palm Springs and asked why he was picking up people on a Saturday afternoon?

His answer was so sweet. He and his wife had been serving the Lord by driving around seeing whom they could help. She had recently passed away, and he continued their service. "I saw you, and I felt I should stop." This made me feel so good. He too had an inner speaking. We rejoiced in the Lord's leading—he taught me that expression.

"Why don't I give you a ride to Palm Springs? It's only about an hour away. The girl should wake up by then." Our charge slept most of the way. She came to when we were in the desert and panicked, thinking we had kidnapped her. I assured her that we meant well and acted in the name of Jesus. It took some convincing to get her name and address. I told her that I would remain in Palm Springs, but that the gentleman would drive her home. I had to make sure that she understood there were no ulterior motives. He was not interested in her other than to take her home. We prayed. I gave her a New Testament, pocket size. I arrived at my destination, and a few days later I received a postcard from my co-worker, "mission accomplished!" What a sweet reward there is in serving! "*I come and my reward is with me.*"

20

Entering a Walk of Service

Hope

Before my month of service was up with the missionary lady, a pastor came. He informed us of a dire need in the community, and asked if I could help after the missionary's husband returned? The need concerned a woman called Hope who was devastated as a result of exceedingly frightful events in her family. Her husband divorced her, and her sixteen-year-old son, under the influence of drugs, had killed a woman and cut up her body with a butcher knife. All this happened behind her back while she was spending her days at the exclusive La Jolla Country Club, north of San Diego. To avoid facing the community after these events, she fled La Jolla with her three daughters. She also needed to find cheaper rent, as her husband had cut off all support. She was now living off the interest of her children's trust fund. The interest amounted to four hundred dollars a month, a drastic drop from her previous lifestyle of a husband's sixty thousand dollars a year. "Would I help her out?" asked the pastor, and in order for it not to be a financial drain, the pastor committed himself to give thirty dollars a month for my food. "*In all your ways acknowledge Me.*"

Two days later I met Hope. She was a tall blond with straight short hair who was obviously distraught. I assured her that I came to bring her comfort and friendship, that I could live with her and her three children as long as was needed, and that I would buy my own food. I moved in, sharing the bedroom with her and the youngest girl. The other two girls slept in the second bedroom. The whole house was sparsely furnished, but we did not care, for we were occupied with more important matters.

Poor Hope. She was overcome with grief, anxiety, and fear. A knock at the door or a ring of the phone would push her panic button. The children were not allowed to leave the house and had not resumed school. They cared for their mother, answering the doorbell or the telephone. To relieve them, I suggested that she release them to go to school. Although it was the school year's end, maybe an exception would be made. The exception was made, and the girls were happy. The other school children knew nothing about this family's tragedies.

Hope was jumpy for some time. She was afraid of her ex-husband and her son. But when the husband never came nor called and when the boy was sent to prison in Tracy, northern California, her fears subsided. We went shopping together, and I showed her how to make her money last longer than ten days, for there were other foods besides lobster, caviar and filet mignon. All children like hamburgers and spaghetti. Then there was rice, beans and whole wheat bread. Plenty of milk, and eggs, and cheese would keep the children happy and healthy. Neighbors supplied us with fruit and vegetables from their gardens. "Look, Hope, we are doing great. The Lord is our supply."

Occasionally we could afford an extra treat, like ice cream. The children stopped taking things for granted and developed an appreciation for many things.

One day we started to talk about the trust fund. The fund and the trustees were in Chicago. I asked her if we could contact them and explain the difficult financial situation. "Those trustees are so old and set in their ways. They won't release anything," she said.

"How about suggesting they look into the matter of buying the children a house, instead of wasting money on rent. Surely they could consider that." We composed the letter, she signed it, and, lo and behold, we received a good response. A trustee was to be in California within the next two months. He would stop by to have a firsthand look at the possibilities of buying a house.

He came while I was still with Hope, and could see the practical need. He left, assuring us that the case would be discussed at the next board meeting. We both said, "Let's wait and see!" We waited a couple of months more before the long-awaited letter came. With the letter in hand, the suspense became even greater: Will it say *yes* or will it say *no*? Hope gave me the letter to open and read, as she was too nervous. With a glance, I could tell her it said *yes!* The money to buy a house was released and a trustee would come and attend to the purchase. It took a tremendous load off of Hope's shoulders as the old gentleman also offered to help monitor the children's education.

The household was in order. Hope had regained her self-control. My job was done, and I felt free to go on. Shortly after, they moved into a very attractive rustic house in Alpine which was near a brook. The children were given a donkey to ride and care for; I shared in their happiness.

Julia

There was an old woman named Julia, ninety-six years of age, who lived in an old cabin close to the center of Alpine. She was as sharp as a tack. She heard and saw everything going on around her. She listened to the news and typed letters on a machine which was every bit as old as she. It only had lower case letters on big round keys, a museum piece, which matched everything else in her cabin. The dishes and utensils in the kitchen were her mother's. Her livelihood came from Social Security; it was not much. Of it, fifteen dollars went for rent, and a little for food. With the balance, she bought second-hand clothes for the war-impoverished people in Europe. Since 1945, she had been mailing them a package every month. Now the clothes collection was getting out of hand as people started to bring more, and she had to stop the mailing because of age and health. Her small bedroom had become a storage room.

Someone suggested I visit her because she also liked to talk about the Lord. Julia was a lively and interesting person. No one could fool her. On one of my visits, I found her sick with bronchitis, and she asked me if I could stay and help her get well. "Let me talk with Hope about this because I am still living with her." That was an excuse. The fact was that the cabin was too dirty, with thick dust everywhere. The walls were blackened and cobwebs were swaying from the ceiling. I always stood up when I visited her and didn't even dare to sit down, let alone come and live in that place.

I cried out, "Lord, if you really want me to live there, You will have to send some angels to clean up and paint that old cabin." Guess what? The painters came the next morning, and took all the furniture outdoors, with Julia on her daybed. They cleaned and painted the front room that doubled as a bedroom and the breakfast nook, where Julia stayed on her daybed. When I came in the late afternoon, I was speechless. "Lord, you really did send the angels–in this case, painters. Now I have no excuse."

"Julia, when would you like me to come and stay with you?" I moved into the front room.

Oh! How I wish I had recorded her long tales spoken in a rough voice with a down-to-earth nineteenth century vocabulary. It was priceless. Sick as she was, spitting green phlegm into a paper bag, she entertained me with stories of her life. Before the Big Fire, she was selling corsets to the farm women around San Francisco, from her horse-drawn wagon. Her little girl went along with her, rain or shine. In 1906, when the great fires of the earthquake blazed around her house, she was prepared, having covered the roof with thick quilts she kept soaking with buckets of water. It was the daughter's job to carry the buckets up the ladder. Every house in the neighborhood burned down but that of Julia and her sixteen year-old helper. I know it for a fact, for she had a news clipping to prove it.

Julia was a strong, courageous, and determined woman, a true pioneer, the kind that built America. Only her heart needed a little push, and she had been taking strychnine daily for the past fifty years for that condition. Who am I to try to change that habit?

However, she said, "Don't you ever give me any penicillin. I lost four friends. They were allergic to it and died."

In spite of my care, she was losing weight. "Julia, I know you won't like it, but I think we should call a doctor." There was one living in Alpine, and he was willing to stop by on his way home from his office in San Diego. It did not take him long to diagnose her condition as double pneumonia.

I whispered to the doctor to please not prescribe penicillin, but she overheard it, and found enough energy to sit up and strongly say, "Don't you give me any penicillin!"

"If she does not take the drug, she will die! Are you going to take such responsibility?"

"But, doctor, aren't there any herbs or other old fashioned remedies that could help her?"

"No!" he said angrily, and packed his black bag to leave.

"How much do we owe you?"

"Five dollars." I paid and he was gone.

"Julia," I said, "you are not going to die. I serve a living God, and I am here to care for the living not the dead. Julia, between me and you and the Lord there will be no death in this house." I spoke with authority from my inner being. The following evening I sensed the angel of death, and I confronted him: "You are not taking Julia. She is mine. The Lord gave her to me." I held her fragile body in my arms, passing vitality to her. Death left.

For several evenings I kept holding her in my arms when her vitality was ebbing. Julia had the will to live. "I have not finished my ministry on earth yet," she said.

Daily, I went in search of fresh fruit and vegetables. It was late fall, and many neighbors had vegetable patches and fruit trees. Everyone knew Julia and gladly supplied the freshest and the best. Half a mile down the road a Czech lady had chickens and goats. I would gather the eggs right out of the nest and buy the morning milk. The woman assured me that when the goat's milk was immediately refrigerated after milking, it had no smell and no identifying taste. I made yogurt and cottage cheese from it. I had to be so careful with my patient not to upset her. Julia had some strong concepts about food. I had to manage to get around them because she had to have good nourishment.

Slowly, she started to recover. One balmy evening she said, "I want to sleep outside!" I was taken aback, never expecting such a wish, but, then, why not? I arranged her day bed under the eucalyptus trees. With assistance she walked the twenty feet to her bed. I used a lounge chair beside her. Eucalyptus has well-known healing properties, especially on breathing. The weather changed the next night, and we did not repeat our outing. Once had been enough to stimulate her recovery.

At times she would try to convince me to become a Mormon. "Why would I want to be a Mormon? I am a Christian, and I serve the living God whom I know. Who is this Angel Moroni? I do not need him, I have the Holy Spirit!" She would get upset and mutter something. Sometimes I would ask her, "Where are your Mormon brothers and sisters? Why don't they take care of you if they are so good? Look, I am not a Mormon, but I am the one who cares for you in the name of the Lord!"

She had to admit it was so. Finally she acknowledged that my God and her God were the same: "We have the same God!" she announced. "Amen!"

I spent my spare time reading the Word, as I had in other places, and now crocheting a white cardigan out of beautiful Priscilla yarn. Priscilla yarn is a fine quality, shining cotton usually used to crochet bedspreads.

Within six weeks Julia had recovered, and her daughter finally came to visit her mother. She was more than amazed to find me attending her. "How did you manage to care for her?"

she asked. "My mother has managed to wear out her welcome with everyone, even the hospital, because within a couple of days she would take charge over the patients, the nurses, and the doctors, telling everyone what to do and how to do the job. How did you manage?"

"I have learned to get the job done without talking about it and not crossing her will. We got along fine because first and foremost we have the Lord!"

Julia's daughter asked me what I was doing in Alpine and told me I belonged in Palm Springs, where she lived with her husband. Then she offered me a ride. I did need to move on. She drove me to a working girl's lodge and gave me fifty dollars, enough to pay a month's rent. "*In all your ways acknowledge Me...Take no thought for your life.*"

Four years later a friend saw Julia on television dancing a jig on her one-hundredth birthday. What a unique character she was, and what a Wonderful God we have!

21

Palm Springs

What a beautiful, clean, and tranquil village was Palm Springs in the winter of '54-'55! Started by Christians as a retreat in the 'thirties, it soon became a favorite place of actors and artists. The old hotel drew an international crowd and was still in use. I walked up and down Canyon Road, the main street, and came across a newly opened dress shop advertising Paris imports. I went in to look around and asked the owner to see the imports. The dresses had not yet arrived—they never did. I told him that I had lived in Paris and knew something about clothes and styles and that I would be willing to work in his shop. He hired me on the spot.

A month later, the dresses had not arrived and, because of advertising, people came asking for them. The owner, a Bulgarian refugee, was trying to sell U.S. made clothes for imports. I could not do it and told him that, *first*, this was not honest and *second*, that the American woman is well informed and would not be fooled. He thought that I was a fool.

When a hefty lady walked in asking to see our collection, I had to tell her that I was sorry but we did not carry her size. "Oh, yes, we can fit you," said the boss, and turning to me, he continued, "Show her our new arrivals." Those new arrivals were circular skirts, in other words, tents; the worst style to put on a large woman. I felt ashamed as I showed her the garment, saying it would not be becoming even after alterations. She left. The boss turned to me and said,

"You are too honest. You cannot take God into business."

"Oh, yes, you can. I had a very successful business based on honesty."

"You are an idiot. I have to let you go."

Since Palm Springs was a winter home to many celebrities who did not like to be seen in public, I thought that a Personal Shopper Service would be an appropriate service to offer. A public secretary on Canyon Road was willing to take my calls and make appointments. I went to the newspaper to put in an advertisement and met up with the social editor. She invited me for lunch to be her guest at the Tennis Club, a socialite hangout, and she wrote a generous article about me in the paper. All this happened within the week!

I waited a week, and only one call came. Distressed, I wondered why there was no response. The inner Voice gave me the answer, "This activity will never satisfy you. You will only be happy in My service." I gave up the activity.

Another week went by, and I received a call from my former employer, yes, the one who had fired me. "I have to leave town for a few days with my partner. Would you come to work while we are gone? Can we talk it over at lunch?"

"No."

He called again.

"No," I again replied. On the third time he pleaded, and I was ready for a good lunch. He came in a flashy red car. "How do you like my new car?"

I wore a lovely raspberry red dress of my own design and making, and so I said, "I don't. It does not match my outfit." I was having fun. "Why do you insist on my coming to work? After all, you called me an idiot."

"I do not trust the girls who are working for me. Money is missing from the cash register. I want you to find out who the culprit is. You believe in God; I can trust you." That was a strange twist!

"All right, but what you really need is a detective. If you want me to do the job, you must pay me detective wages, twenty-five dollars a day." The man did not like this but had to agree. I was given one key to open one lock, and the manager had the other key for the second lock. The partners did not trust one another either, and one could not get in the store without the other!

Seemingly, I was to help with the inventory. The two salesgirls were of the good old American moral stock. I did not suspect any of them. I asked myself, "Why is money missing?"

As we started work on the second day, the manager became very angry with me, "You came to spy on us. You padded the cash register. It was twenty dollars over last night."

I assured her that I did not do it and did not have twenty dollars to risk. "I do not know what happened, but let us see what turns up tonight." That night after the salesgirls had gone home, the manager and I counted the money from the register, but according to the sales slips, some money was missing.

I told her, "I am your friend and I believe you are innocent. Let me add up all your receipts from the past few days, but, not on the register. I can add just as fast in my head." My addition did not correspond with the cash register, but it did correspond with the money received.

"Let us check with some of the other days when you had to make up the difference out of your own pocket," I suggested. The same thing occurred; the register did not correspond to the receipts. It became apparent to me, that when the money in the register totaled more than the receipts, the boss probably said nothing to the girls, but that when the register money totaled less than the receipts, the girls had to pay the balance.

On the third morning we told the girls about the faulty register. They were relieved, but I was angry. The boss surely knew! When he returned, I made certain he heard the story in detail, "I am happy to inform you that you can trust the girls, but not the register. We checked on the past receipts; the register is faulty."

The man became angry and upset. "Pay her off," he told the manager.

"How much?" the manager asked.

"A dollar an hour. Three days, twenty-four dollars."

"Oh, no," said I. "We agreed on twenty-five a day. I did the job. Three days, seventy five dollars."

"Give it to her," and turning to me the boss said, "The trouble with you, is that you are a very intelligent girl."

"Last time, you called me an idiot" I said. "God is righteous." I took my much needed check and saw him no more.

A Testimony

On my first Sunday morning in Palm Springs, I was longing to meet people who knew the Lord, so I went early to the Community Church and sat on a bench waiting for the doors to open. My heart was open to the Lord, who said, "You may attend but do not join." Many came to the service. There was much singing, reading, and speaking, but nothing really touched me. The pastor seemed to be a very kind and personable man. At the end of the service, an announcement was made about the Christmas program and about the volunteer help that would be needed. I was glad to offer my services. We were to present a pageantry of living *tableaux (pictures)* of the life of Jesus. I was given charge of the costumes.

My friend Nadia from New York, with whom I had joined the Theosophical Society, had moved to Tucson, a mere four hundred miles from Palm Springs. She had shown me her sumptuous collection of oriental fabrics, some with silver and gold threads. I could use them in the *tableaux*!

There was another major reason I wanted to go to Tucson. Nadia had not experienced the revelation of Jesus, and I desired to witness to her that God had brought me through the veil, and that it had pleased the Father to reveal to me His Son! Jesus was real!

One morning by the pool, I spoke of my desire to go to Tucson to another happy lodge-dweller relaxing in the sun. "Let's go. I have a car," she said. We were off in fifteen minutes. In another ten minutes on the road, she reached for her purse and pulled out a flask of whiskey.

"You are not going to continue to drink and drive, are you?"

"No," she said, "You drive."

"I do not know how."

"There is nothing to it. Just put it in drive and give it gas." She exited the car, came to the passenger side and said, "Move over." I had no choice. Indeed, it seemed safer for me to drive. Nothing to it! We were on a deserted desert road. After I developed the feel of the car, I drove a steady sixty miles per hour until nightfall. I learned quickly to drive forward and to slow down before a sharp turn, after skidding on the first one!

We stopped overnight in a motel and visited Nadia the next day. She gladly let me borrow some fabrics and invited us to spend the day and the night with her, but I had one more burden to share and came to the point.

"Nadia," I said, "Christ is the answer to our search!" Yet I could not bring her to see that Jesus had to die and shed His blood to redeem us sinners. She could not accept, in her words, "this bloody and gory sacrifice." She could not love a God that required such an offering. "Besides, the Bible is written by man," she said.

I was not about to enter into a heated argument. I had a red-letter Bible with me. "All right. Let us read the red-letter passages. They are the recorded words spoken by Jesus." I read: "*Jesus said, I am the way, the truth, and the life—no one comes to the Father but through me—I am the door—I am the living Water—I am the bread of life—You are bought with my precious blood, you are not your own....*" I read on and on. She could not accept the message of salvation. That was that. The Lord had made a way for me to bring her the good news of salvation and a message of hope, but she did not receive it, at least not then. I never did see her again. I returned the fabrics by mail.

We spent the rest of the day in the indescribably inspiring Tucson desert. Before leaving, I presented Nadia with my red-letter Bible, encouraging her to find out more about Jesus' speaking. My companion, sobered by the reading of the Word, was quiet and relaxed. She insisted I drive back to Palm Springs, for practice's sake.

A Baptism

On the road, I shared with my companion my desire to be baptized by immersion . "Oh," she said, "I belong to a Baptist Church in Van Nuys. You can be baptized there. Come with me to Van Nuys over a weekend." We went, and on a Sunday morning after the service, I approached a group of preachers and told them of my desire to be baptized. "Could you baptize me now since I came from out of town?" I asked.

"Why do you want to be baptized?"

"Because I read that Jesus was immersed in a river, and He also said, 'Follow me and you shall be my disciples.' I want to be a disciple."

They looked at one another perplexed and finally said, "All right." I was put into the water in the name of the Father and the Son and the Holy Spirit. It was simple. No more questions were asked; nothing more was said. I felt happy inside because I had obeyed the Word even though I understood little of what had happened. But it is written, "*He that believes and is baptized shall be saved.*"

A Pageantry

Back in Palm Springs, under the spirited leadership of a young lady, the Christmas program was taking shape. She was well known in town and her enthusiasm inspired cooperation. The backdrop of the *tableau* was painted by a Hollywood professional. The music was composed for the occasion by another talented person of the Palm Springs colony. The pastor wrote and read the script with the corresponding Bible verses. It was a big production.

We concentrated on six *tableaux*, including the trip to Bethlehem, the Nativity scene, the shepherds in the field, and the three Wise Men. For the fifth scene I suggested reading Isaiah's prophesy: "*Unto us a child is born, unto us a son is given; and the government shall be upon his shoulders; and his name is called Wonderful, Counselor, Mighty God, Eternal Father, and Prince of Peace.*" The sixth *tableau* was to be of Christ's return.

For this, I asked all the participants in the scenes to come costumed on stage and to stand facing the sky-painted backdrop, with their hands lifted up in praise. A small light was projected and shined upon their faces. And in addition, a strong light was reflected by a cross-shaped mirror to project a cross upon the darkened sky. It was very effective, mysterious, and inspiring.

Having to dress and arrange the people in the *tableaux*, I remained behind the scene and could not see the congregation. Nevertheless, I was praying all the time; "Lord, bless the audience. Speak to the people." Since I could not hear a sound coming from them, I even wondered if anyone had come. I was assured by others that the hall was full. I realized then that there was a holy hush under the Spirit of the Lord. The audience was very moved by this presentation. "Thank You, Lord, for Your presence."

A week later, I was asked to thank a Christian lawyer from the congregation for his community participation. When I went to see him, I was struck by the thousands of books lining the walls of his office. Setting my small Bible on his desk, I pointed to the law books and said, "To think that all we need to know is in this little Book!" He nodded and said, "You are right, but..."

"Yes, but... but few read it, less believe it, and even fewer put it into practice!" I left and thought, "Lord, thy Kingdom come to earth as it is in heaven!"

22

The Seminary

An evangelist came to Palm Springs and spoke on redemption and on the meaning of receiving the Lord, that is, being born again. I saw that this is what had happened to me in Alpine. I came forward at the altar call to make a public declaration. Ladies from the Baptist Church of Bellflower had come with the young evangelist. They welcomed me and invited me for lunch.

My zeal for the Lord was evident, and when they found out my precarious financial condition—the seasonal dress shop where I was working was about to close—they asked me to come to Bellflower as a guest. It was very heartwarming.

Sunday after Sunday, the pastor of a Baptist Church was preaching on the book of John. He spoke on Jesus being the door, the living water and the bread of life. I could relate to this living speaking and was taking it all in. The hymns were particularly touching. Oh, how I liked to sing—still off key—about the "*Precious, precious blood of Jesus, ever flowing free*," "*I know that my Redeemer liveth*," and "*Trust and obey: for there's no other way*." One hymn was specifically directed toward consecration: "*Take my life and let it be, consecrated, Lord, to Thee*." All those hymns penetrated my being. They were real.

The Lord gave me one specific hymn to keep singing and singing:

When I survey the wondrous cross
On which the Prince of Glory died,
My richest gain I count but loss,
And pour contempt on all my pride.

Forbid it, Lord, that I should boast,
Save in the death of Christ, my God;
All the vain things that charm me most,
I sacrifice them to His blood.

Were the whole realm of nature mine,
That were an offering far too small:
Love so amazing, so divine,
Demands my soul, my life, my all.[1]

The Bellflower ladies took good care of me, and we met often for Bible studies. One of them had a Thompson Chain Reference Bible, which was very complete and attracted my desire to learn. I expressed the wish of obtaining one.

"This is just for those who want to study for the ministry. You are zealous now, but you will cool off in time." I was shocked. I did not ever want to cool off, and some day I would buy the Bible. Because I was asked to give my testimony here and there, I received generous love offerings.

By September, the Baptist ladies decided to send me to the Theological Seminary in Covina. They would pay for my tuition. *Me?* In a seminary? How did I deserve such an honor? The Christian walk was completely foreign to me, I did not know how to react or what to say. I just followed, walking through the open doors, as my Master had instructed.

Reading the Book daily and not understanding much, I knew I had much to learn. The dean needed to know something about me in order to direct me to the proper classes. We had a short conversation, and he suggested I take the general curriculum plus a class on the Old Testament and one on philosophy. The hour long class on philosophy was to be my first and my last. The opening words were: "God being invisible and dwelling in unapproachable light, we cannot know Him." *What?* We cannot know God? I could not sit still. "But, sir, I came here to find out about God. Is this not the purpose of this seminary? This morning I read, '*God wants all men to be saved and come to the full knowledge of Him.*' In Colossians it says that '*we will come to the full knowledge of the mystery of God, Christ!*' " And, "*Blessed are the pure in heart for they shall see God.*"

I had said enough and sat down immersed in my own thoughts. I was here to learn, to know more about God. I knew Him a little; I wanted more. I had given up everything in life to be told that God dwelled in unapproachable light? No, no, no! Yes, He dwells there, but He also dwells in my heart, and in His Word. This was a fact; this was real. I had experienced Him many times.

The dean called me that afternoon. "Helena, you would probably be happier in a class other than philosophy. You have already had enough of it in the past. How about taking church administration and government?"

"All right."

After the third class on delegation of authority, the teacher showed us the perpendicular way of its distribution, such as in the Catholic Church. It was a pyramid from the Pope to the cardinals, to the bishops, to the fathers, to the little people. I had been one of those little ones, crushed at the bottom. The other delegation was a horizontal one, from the pastor, to the deacons and people, such as in Protestantism. I listened carefully. This still was the clergy and laity system. I asked, "Where does the Holy Spirit come into this?" The answer was that the Holy Spirit was ten percent of the work, and ninety percent was up to the hardworking clergy. I kept quiet, not being able to answer, but I was not happy.

In the Old Testament class I unintentionally confronted the teacher. We were studying the kings and the prophets before and during the captivity. "Sir, being almost twice the age of the other students, I have a hard time remembering all those strange names which I have never heard before. The stories are interesting, but what is the point?" I vented my feelings in front of the class, meaning no harm. I asked the teacher to show us how it all related to us today, how it helped us in our daily life. I told him that I was simply too old for stories without a purpose. No clear answer was given, and the lecture went on as usual. In other words, this was only a historical record of the Jews, and we had to know it.

One young girl befriended me. For a long time, she was a welcome companion, until I realized that my love for her was running out. I was bothered by my selfishness. "Lord, I am short on love. I need more love." Little by little my attitude changed. He was answering, "*Love does not find fault; love covers a multitude of sins. Friendship does not expose; friendship covers. I love Him, because He loved me first!*" At that time I discovered First Corinthians 13, the chapter on love. I read it over and over, filling my loneliness and emptiness by the comfort in those words.

I noticed that my clothes that I had carried from Alpine were becoming shabby. "Lord, how about a change of clothes?" Not three days went by when a lady brought me an old grocery box of clothes that I could either keep or pass on. I did not like what I saw. The colors were washed out, the blacks were gray, the whites were gray, and so on. "Lord! Do I have to look like a mouse to serve You?" I closed the box and gave it away. "If I serve You, I want to serve You *first class*." Within a week I received another beautiful giftbox with clothes in luscious colors. "Thank You! This is more like it!"

On Sundays, we went to the First Baptist Church in Pomona to worship. The brother of our dean conducted the service. I was asked to give my testimony to a large group of young executives at the Sunday school class. We had a Sunday school text to follow, and then, I spoke from my heart of the Lord's speaking, guiding, and being real to me. The class asked their regular teacher to have me teach them. He refused. He happened to be my Old Testament teacher! Was I glad he refused! I had little knowledge to go on. What could I teach? However, I kept being asked to give my testimony in surrounding churches and was given love offerings. In my testimony, I never went as far as to tell of my experience of having 'been slain.' I felt an inward check.

I had come to the seminary with many questions, the first and the foremost being, "Where is the Kingdom of God? I am a new Christian, and I am looking for the kingdom." There were only blank faces. Then I asked them, "You mean to say you have been praying for two thousand years: 'Thy kingdom come!' and no kingdom?" I expected to find some Christians living in a kingdom here on earth. Not knowing God before, I thought that I had missed the land and I wanted to know where Christians lived together. No one had the answer.

Then I asked about healing. The four Gospels showed Jesus going about healing the sick. How about us? No answer. And so on and so on. What was going on? I was only innocently asking things according to the black and white word of the Bible.

The year came to an end. At the office I was asked, "Would you like to take a job?"

"Yes, but it depends on what kind."

"There is a need for a dormitory mother at Girls' Town in Arlington, by Riverside."

"I'd like to look into it. I desire to serve the Lord."

I took the job and left the seminary somewhat empty inside. There were now even more unanswered questions. Was it a waste of time? As a matter of fact, my Old Testament teacher was to be my New Testament teacher the following year. As I was leaving for summer vacation, he said, "I probably cannot answer your questions. I think you will waste your time if you return here next year." Oh great! What is a theological seminary for? Someone called them cemeteries. Indeed, my living Jesus was being pushed out of the way, buried, replaced by intellectual reasonings and historical knowledge. In His mercy, the Lord left me with a deep yearning to know the full truth and He gave me a revelation, "*I love Him, because He loved me first.*"

23

Girls' Town

Having read about Boys' Town, I thought I had some idea about what Girls' Town would be like. I did sense an inward prompting and accepted the job, which provided room and board and pocket money. Before becoming a Girls' Town, the place was an abandoned Army camp. All the buildings were barracks. There were about twelve of them. The girls, ages six to sixteen, came from broken homes, from parents in jail, from the street, or from juvenile courts. There were sixty-five girls in all, living in six barracks, according to age.

Being a relief housemother, I slept in a different barrack every night, but on the seventh, I had my own room which I could furnish very attractively from donated things. On the door I put up a sign: "*Knock and it shall be opened.*" On my desk the sign read: "*Ask and you shall receive.*" However, I did not put up all of the verse: "*Seek and you shall find*" was too risky. It could invite trouble as a number of the girls had been in the juvenile system for robbery. The Lord was with me every step of the way. At the seminary it seemed as if He were hiding, but here His presence was so prevalent. The job was a breeze.

My work put me in contact with all the girls, and we had a couple of hours together before bedtime. The first week they looked me over. The second, they tried to see what they could get away with. On the third week I was tipped off that the older girls in barrack number six were planning to gang up on me. "What do we do, Lord?"

"Treat them with kindness," was the speaking.

Deciding on an ice cream party, I cleared my plan with the office and obtained permission for a girl to go out and buy some ice cream. Entering the barrack, before anyone had time to start anything, I said, "Girls, there is a surprise for you tonight. Something you all like. Guess what?" They were curious, but could not guess, because to buy ice cream you had to leave the premises, and they thought it could not be done.

"You select one girl we can all trust," I told them. We came to a unanimous agreement. I gave her money and revealed the secret. She had permission to buy ice cream for our party, only she had to report to the office upon going and coming back. Was everybody happy! They all began arranging their gear for the party. The venom had left this bunch of sixteen-year-olds who had known, witnessed, or participated in every possible vice.

This event was the turning point in the camp for me. I was tested and approved by the girls. They gave me their confidence, saying "You are real; you are not a fake." Actually, it was the Lord's love flowing out of me, and I received the credit.

We had rules and regulations posted all over the camp. "Don't do this. Don't do that. Don't...Don't...Don't..." I put colorful notices in the barracks. "Think of all the fun and good times you can have in coming to pick fruit and berries, in learning to knit and crochet, in being orderly and on time." I changed the don'ts into do's. Here was an example of the *true* positive thinking that I was learning from the Lord. This was in contrast to the human way of positive thinking which I had practiced in New York and which finally came to an end, for it was by the strength and will of man rather than under the guidance of God.

I came to love those girls, and they loved me. They were willing participants in some extra-curricular activities such as knitting and crocheting, and fruit and berry picking. The berries grew in abundance on the land. We had a good time.

One day I was most surprised to receive a letter from the dean of the seminary I had attended. The office had informed him that I owed six months' tuition. The bill was enclosed. I had wondered why there was no word from the Baptist ladies. They had stopped payment without advising me or giving a reason. The office had not told me either. The dean wrote some sharp words and expected me to rapidly settle my account. Earlier, my young student friend in the seminary had gently warned me that the speaking on campus was that I was a Communist. The student body and the faculty were all involved. I had at first dismissed it as gossip. Now, I realized what proportions it had taken. Behind my back a storm had been brewing. The accusations and evil speaking obviously had reached my Bellflower lady friends who, as a result, had cut their support.

Having received this letter, I asked, "Lord, what do we do about this?" This was preposterous. Me, a Communist? I felt at peace and slept soundly that night until three in the morning. The faithful voice of my *Advocate* was dictating a letter. I rose up and wrote as fast as I could, to the effect that I was a White Russian, that my family had fought Communism and lost their country, their fortune, and their fame in the process. Besides, I was a born-again Christian. How could I possibly be for a Godless country? I owe you and the seminary nothing. You owe me for character assassination and defamation. There was more to the letter which I cannot recall. The letter hit home. By return mail I received a deep apology from the dean. He acknowledged that he had been absent too many times and not in contact with the students. My debt was erased. Thank you, Lord!

At Girls' Town the services had been Pentecostal. The preaching had more fervor than content. The strange tongues turned me off. I had had plenty of time there to read the Bible profusely. One house mother who was always carrying the Good Book asked me, "What do you want from the Lord?"

"I do not know."

"You must want to be an overcomer!" That struck a chord in me, and I went for my Thompson Reference Bible, which I had acquired. The reference led me to the book of Revelation and I glanced at it. This was a mysterious book! I started reading from the first chapter and was encouraged by verse 3: "*Blessed is he that readeth, and they that hear the words of this prophecy, and keep those things which are written therein: for the time is at hand.*" I was attracted by the words of these three chapters and read them repeatedly, although I did not understand the meaning.

What was the *tree of life* in Chapter 2:7? Or the *second death* in 2:11? Or the *white stone* in 2:17? I liked reading that the overcomers will have power over the nations (2:26), of having their names confessed before the Father (3:5), of having the name of God and of the New Jerusalem written on them (3:12), and finally, of sitting on Christ's throne (3:20).

Within me something was swelling up, satisfying me, making me happy. Hallelujah! Then I also felt the need for more cleansing. I was singing the hymns about the cross and the blood and decided to take communion all by myself. "Lord, I cannot get enough of your cleansing blood." Prayerfully, and sip by sip, I would drink a whole glass of grape juice and sing *my* song:

When I survey the wondrous cross
On which the Prince of Glory died,
My richest gain I count but loss,
And pour contempt on all my pride.
...Love so amazing, so divine,
Demands my soul, my life, my all.

Since my conversion I had lost interest in most worldly things, in makeup, in the styles of clothes, in the art of living, and in arts and music, because I realized it was emptiness and vanity. I had experienced some of this emptiness in the past, to the point of contemplating suicide. Now I knew why. My inner being had been yearning for the eternal God. At the time of my conversion I tasted the incomparable beauty of the realm of God, and now my whole being was intent on having more of God and less of the world.

Six months into my work I was called by the founder of Girls' Town. She wanted to find out if I knew someone with enough "gray matter" to take over the management of the camp, as she was hoping to retire. I answered that I did not know of anyone. The Lord gave *her* that commission and one cannot retire from the service of the Lord.

On leaving her, I realized that she was trying to bait me, thinking that I was planning a takeover, seeing my success with the girls. She had been uncomfortable. "Lord, as much as I love these girls, I do not want this camp. It could hold a hundred, but we only have sixty-five. This is like serving you sixty-five percent, I want to serve you one hundred percent." My superintendent told me, "Helena, you are running a camp within the camp." I guessed the founder took it as competition. Indeed I was running the Lord's camp among devils.

Not too much time elapsed before the Lord spoke, "Walk through the open doors!" Three days later I understood the speaking and was prepared to hear that I was dismissed for "running a camp within a camp" and for being a Communist! This time the insult did not even matter, considering the source. The door was open, and I was ready to go. An invitation was waiting from a lady who had heard me testify. "Any time you need a place to stay, let me know and I'll come to pick you up." I called. She came right away from Whittier—a dear Christian lady, Dorothy, with whom I had a home for some time.

Having forgotten several things at Girls' Town, I had to go back for them. On the day I returned, it was lunch time, and all of the girls and the staff, including the founder, were in the dining room. As I entered, the girls stood up in unison and gave me a thundering applause. I sent them kisses and went to the table where the staff were sitting, open-mouthed. The superintendent told me that this had never happened before, and for me it was the greatest gratification. The Lord did the work, and I received the praise! "*Vengeance is mine; I will repay!*"

My next stop on the journey to God's sphere was amongst the Pentecostals. Dorothy, my Whittier friend, took me. They insisted on my speaking in tongues. It sounded like meaningless chatter. How could the repetition of a few syllables constitute a language? To satisfy them and to be received, I complied and repeated what I was hearing. But to the Lord I said, "Please, if You have something to tell me, give it to me straight. You can say it in one of the five languages I still remember: Russian, German, French, Czech, or English, but this jabbering I do not understand." We were told to read 1 Corinthian, chapter 12. However, I saw that the speaking in tongues mentioned there is the least of the gifts.

There was much preaching on the baptism of the Holy Ghost, resulting in the speaking in tongues, and they said that without this speaking you were not saved. I knew differently. I knew I was saved, and the small but clear inner voice was confirming it. The Apostle Paul said he would rather speak five words with his understanding that he might teach others also, than ten thousand words in an unknown tongue. He said this in 1 Corinthians, chapter 14 while addressing the same people.

There were other gifts to concentrate on and develop. I strongly believed that the Lord could heal in the present time, as He had done in Galilee. By faith, I exercised the gift of healing. A line of people formed during a healing service, and I prayed for them, with visible results. The following week the same people were in line with another healer. "What is this, Lord? Did You not honor my faith and theirs?"

The answer came: "*They go back to their same ways of life as the sow returns to her wallow.*" I could see that healing the body was not the answer, but that the soul needed an inward healing. I stopped exercising my gift in such a public way; however, time and again, on a one-to-one basis, the Lord would stir in me to pray for the healing of this or that one. I witnessed dramatic miracles.

One of these miracles happened in a small church in Bellflower. A man on crutches came to be prayed for. I was there with three preachers. "Pray for him, Helena. He has been coming to be healed for years," said the Pentecostal pastor in a *get rid of him* voice. I went to the man. We prayed, and from deep within I said, "By the name and power of the Lord Jesus, be healed." The man, after sixteen years on crutches, dropped them and walked out, as straight as could be. Sheepishly, the pastor picked up the crutches. He could not claim the credit. He ignored me. The glory belongs only to the Lord! Amazing!

The preaching among the Pentecostals was loud and emotional. I tried to imitate them but couldn't. I could not make heads nor tails of their speaking. Most messages had no beginning, no ending. I would ask, "What are you trying to do? What are you building? What is the foundation? What is the basis? What is the goal?" There was no answer.

I continued, however, to love and read the Bible. I didn't understand the differences, connection, or meaning of the two testaments. But as I read on, more pieces of the puzzle fell into place. Occasionally, something of the New Testament was clarified by the Old, or vice versa. Was I thrilled then! Isaiah was one of those books where I could see a definite connection to the New Testament.

Some Pentecostal Shenanigans

A few Pentecostal preachers talked about the New Jerusalem, a golden city, which was foursquare and built of pure gold, coming down from heaven. "You mean that you *believe* that a huge cube of fifteen hundred miles will descend on the earth?" I asked.

"Yes!"

"How could that be?" I inquired. "That would throw the earth off kilter. God is not interested in bricks of gold but in *people*, in the *church of the Firstborn*. That is what is written in Hebrews 12:22. The Lord will come down from heaven with His elect when He returns." My speaking dropped like a lead weight.

I prayed sincerely, "Lord, keep me from making a fool of myself by defiling Your Word."

There were a few anointed preachers in the Pentecostal churches in the greater Los Angeles area and many sincere believers. As a whole, however, there was no consistency; the presentation of the Word was ambiguous and without continuity. The private lives of many were shocking. As a result, my recollection of Pentecostalism in the late 'fifties was very negative.

At one point, I attended a three-month training on the gifts of the Holy Ghost and Pentecostal practices. Three important incidents, during that training, gave me insight into the "shenanigans" behind many of the Pentecostal practices.

In one of the congregations I attended, there was a painted backdrop behind the speaker's platform, outlining the city of Jerusalem. Painted into it was an oversized portrait of the preacher. During some of the Sunday services a light would appear at the right hand corner of the backdrop and travel ever so slowly to the left. When the service ended at midday the light had reached the center of the stage over the preacher's head. After the meeting people would remark about this heavenly wonder, believing it to be heavenly approval.

During the meetings, I watched this phenomenon carefully and soberly. By the third time, I realized what was happening and quickly went to the parking lot to understand the source of the light. Sure enough, a car reflecting the sun sent its rays through the window and onto the painting. As the sun proceeded from east to west, that is, from left to right, the reflection on the backdrop traveled from right to left. By noon, the light shone in the middle over the preacher's head! Even though we had a class every day, no one parked on this spot during the week. No car, no light! I tried to show the phenomenon to the students, but they only became angry and called me an infidel.

The second incident was one of high-pitched excitement. One morning, when we came to class, there were blood stains on a side aisle and the immediate interpretation by the people was: "Jesus came at night and left His footprints!" So much commotion followed. It was viewed as a special blessing. "Lord," I asked, "what is this?" I did see the blood stains, and they were too close together to have been left by a grown man. I followed them to the stairway leading to the office where the steps stopped. I went upstairs and asked the girls about the blood stains. "Oh!" one of them said. "A little boy cut his toe and came up for a bandage. We cleaned up the steps but not the aisle." I informed the class about the true explanation of the apparent "miracle." This time, the reaction was just short of being violent. I was accused of not believing in miracles. Two women pushed and pulled me down the aisle and outside. As they went back to their seat, I returned to mine to show them that I was not intimidated and that I *did* believe in miracles—when real. "Would the Lord leave His precious blood on a dirty aisle?" I asked. There was silence.

The third instance was the final straw. A building program for a new church was in progress, and I received an offer by letter to inscribe my name in gold on the sky blue dome among the hundred and forty-four thousand for a donation of *one hundred dollars*! "What?" I was incensed. How low and how cheap can you get? I could not get out of town fast enough and went to a friend in San Diego. "Lord, I have never met up with so many demons in my life. Is there something wrong with me?"

Despite my negative experiences, I must make mention of two sincere prophets that I encountered in the Pentecostal movement. One of them, a minister in the San Fernando Valley, prophesied over me by the anointing and said, "The Lord will make you a pillar in the temple of God!" The other, a poor man living in a cabin near Riverside tending to his small garden, looked up at me and said, "You shall be blessed. You shall eat from the Head!" Inwardly, I understood it to mean that I would eat of Christ. Both prophecies gave me hope and encouragement. Years later, these prophecies are still coming to pass.

24

Isaiah

My daily needs were met as doors were opened to me to care for others: the poor, the sick, the newborn, the old. I always offered my help free of charge and the grateful families gave me room and board in return. I served them in the name of the Lord. I slept anywhere; it did not matter.

By that time I had completely recovered; my nerves were steady and my mind clear. One verse was particularly helpful in overcoming my fears and anxieties. I would quote it in times of need: "*For God has not given (me) the spirit of fear but of POWER (over my anxieties) of LOVE (towards people and the environment) and of a SOUND MIND*" (2 Tim. 1:7). This verse sustained me for a long time. The compassionate God, through the Word, His presence, and His anointing was my constant companion. When I transgressed, He was merciful to bring me back.

In my spare time, I would avidly read the Word for hours, as I mentioned before. The book of Isaiah captivated me in those days. "*Come now, and let us reason together....Though your sins be as scarlet, they shall be as white as snow; though they be red like crimson, they shall be as wool. If you be willing and obedient, you shall eat the good of the land,*" (Isaiah 1:18-19).

"*The Lord that made (me) and formed (me) from the womb will help (me)*" (Isaiah 44:2). "*I have even called you! I have surnamed you though you have not known me"* (45:4). *"Fear not, you worm Jacob for I am with you." "...be not dismayed; for I am your God: I will strengthen you, yea, I will help you, yea, I will uphold you with the right hand of my righteousness"* (41:14,10). I recalled my experience in Alpine when seeing myself as a worm; I had lain prostrate before the Almighty at the time of my salvation and, before that, in a California trailer, when He called me by name and I thought it was a guru speaking to me. Forgive me, Lord.

I applied all of these verses to myself in a personal way, and drew strength, comfort, satisfaction, and hope from them. My love-starved, lonely soul was finally healing. Having lived on my own, determining the course of my own life for so many years, I had unknowingly built a wall of self-reliance, which now began to crumble. I had finally found the personal God that I had been searching for. I would cry over the "*man of sorrows*" who was "*acquainted with grief*" in chapter fifty-three of Isaiah and I would "*draw water with joy out of the wells of salvation*" in chapter twelve. I let these words sink into my heart. What love! A love beyond my grasp.

And then, there are the heart-gripping, triumphant last chapters beginning with chapter sixty. "*Arise and shine, for your light has come and the glory of the Lord has risen upon you....The Spirit of the Lord God is upon me....to proclaim the acceptable year....to give beauty for ashes, the oil of joy for mourning, the garment of praise for the spirit of heaviness....For Zion's sake I will not hold my peace....You shall no more be termed Forsaken; neither shall your land be termed Desolate....For behold, I create new heavens and a new earth....be glad and rejoice for ever in that which I create....Thus said the Lord, the heaven is my throne and the earth is my footstool....but to this man will I look who is of a poor and contrite spirit and trembles at my word....Let the Lord be glorified.*" Of course, there is so much more.

There are also the tremendous prophecies regarding the Messiah. Isaiah whetted my appetite concerning the promises of a Savior. This is not a Bible study, but a recollection of a few revelations which have brought much joy in my life and hope for the second coming of our Lord and King.

Isaiah tells us of a virgin who would conceive and bear a son and call him Emmanuel. Matthew tells us of the event: "*A virgin shall be with child and shall bring forth a son, and they shall call his name Emmanuel, God with us.*" Isaiah continues, "*Unto us a son is born, unto us a child is given and the government shall be upon his shoulders; and his name shall be called Wonderful, Counselor, The mighty God The everlasting Father, the Prince of Peace.*" Jesus told Philip, "*If you have seen me, you have seen the Father, for the Father and I are one.*"

In Isaiah, I saw Christ being the Son, the Father, and the Counselor or Guide, which according to John 16:13 is the Holy Spirit. The three are one and the same. This was a tremendous revelation which kept me from diverse sects and denominations, which do not believe that Christ is God. My vision was clear. "*In Him (Christ) dwelleth all the fullness of the Godhead bodily*" (Col. 2:9).

Several pieces of the puzzle came together! Christ was all three. He was and is God, Emmanuel God with us. This is a mystery. I had been so impressed by verse 6 of chapter nine of Isaiah since even the first year of my conversion, that I had incorporated the prophet reading his prophecy in the pageantry *tableau* while in Palm Springs. Several years later in Lancaster, California, I was asked to design a float for a Christmas parade. Isaiah had been in the court of the king, so *my* prophet read from a scroll to his immediate entourage on the float, which consisted of members of the court as well as the shepherd boys, indicating that the Word transcended class distinctions. A concealed microphone conveyed the message to the crowds as the procession proceeded through town. "Isaiah" read the message over and over: "*For unto us a child is born, unto us a son is given: and the government shall be upon His shoulder: and His name shall be called Wonderful, Counselor, The Mighty God, The everlasting Father, The Prince of Peace.*" I was searching for a

Kingdom people and purposed to draw attention to the Lord's coming government, when, "*The government shall be upon His shoulder.*"

Such was His plan for my life, at least, in the beginning of my Christian walk. I seldom had money, yet never lacked bread. It had become very clear to me from the day of my conversion that my life's "vocation" was to serve the Lord. I was unencumbered by family responsibilities or possessions. To merely get a job to pay rent, buy food or invest for the future no longer had any meaning for me. From the beginning, the Lord told me to keep my head in the clouds, my feet on the ground and meet the needs at my left hand and my right hand. I continued to live like a sparrow and grow as a lily.

A woman, from the Pentecostal group that I had known, had a verse for me: "*For our light affliction, which is but for a moment, works for us a far more exceeding and eternal weight of glory!*" This verse comforted me exceedingly.

However, I still asked, "where were my teachers?" I continued to seek and investigate one congregation after another as my social work took me to diverse parts of southern California and to all sorts of denominations.

Then sings my soul,
my Savior God to Thee,
How great Thou art,
How great Thou art![2]

25

Searching for Gold

I was so intent on helping to bring about the Kingdom on earth. In one of my many moves, I met a Christian man who taught me how to dowse for water with a willow branch. He told me that I could use the same technique on minerals. This gave me a new idea that I should look for gold to help finance the Kingdom. I knew that the news of the Kingdom had to be preached unto the whole earth, and then the end would come. I had yet to hear any Christian or minister voicing this truth, so I thought *I* could help by at least providing some financing and *the Lord* would provide the preacher.

Turned off by the denominations, I went to Arizona, looking for gold. The Lord spoke, "While you are looking for gold out there, I will work the gold into you."

I had a rod made of copper wire—copper being a good conductor of electricity—attached to a spring and a willow handle. Every element emits radiation to a greater or lesser degree. By clearing your mind and intently concentrating on the mineral you intend to find, you can "tune in" and respond to its vibrations. The rod you are holding will oscillate in the presence of the object if in sizable quantity. This is known as dowsing, or radioesthesia, and you can join the members of its club in London, England, provided you can prove your talent by obtaining commercial results. The man who initiated me to this endeavor had opened a number of oil wells in the Bakersfield area in the mid to late '50's.

Drought was bringing Arizona to the brink of disaster when I came there, and President Eisenhower was on his way to see it for himself. What could he do more than we? Only God can change an Act of God, and He changed it to another Act. After the drought came the floods. Torrential rains welcomed the President's arrival. He turned around and went home. At the time of the floods, I was in a hunter's cabin with other people in rugged country an hour's drive from Payson. The two brooks crossing the road to the village became turbulent rivers. There was no way out and no way in. My gold hunting was rained out, washed out! But I had my knitting and my Bible, with a great many references.

The area was known for semi-precious stones, and looking out the window, I could see a mountain of red jasper. I felt an inner stirring and was reminded that jasper was mentioned in Revelation. I looked up the references. The first mention was in chapter 4: "*He (God) who sat on the throne appeared like jasper.*" Later in the New Jerusalem, the wall was jasper, the foundation was jasper, and "her light like unto a stone most precious, even like a jasper stone, clear as crystal." I was told of a transparent green jasper. This was certainly different, for the jasper in front of me was opaque, semi-precious and red.

What was the message? I did not receive the interpretation until later. God formed Adam out of dust, actually out of red clay, Adam meaning *red clay* in Hebrew.

Under God's appointed pressures of life, my red clay was turning to semi-precious stone, but that was not good enough. To be part of the New Jerusalem I needed much more transformation. I needed to be transparent, precious, crystal clear and green. "Only You, Lord, can accomplish such a feat of skill!"

Days went by. The water was rising higher, and the food supply was dropping lower. I used the last drop of cream in my morning coffee and jokingly said: "Lord, the cream is gone. Will You command some ravens to feed us like You did with Elijah?" And what do you suppose happened? In the distance among the trees and the forest I saw a tree trunk moving! I shook my head. Was I seeing a vision? In a few moments a man showed up in his brownish-green rainwear that matched the trees.

We were astounded. He had managed to cross the first brook in the jeep and had to leave the vehicle behind at the second brook, crossing it on foot, fighting the treacherous and churning waters. There was food in his back pack: "I did not want you to run out of milk and cream," he said laughingly. "Lord, you are too much! You did send a raven. What kindness, what a sense of humor! How can we not love You?"

I spent that summer in Payson, Arizona, working in a coffee shop enjoying the rugged folks and the majestic sunsets. Under the luscious green of the Arizona pines there was a motel consisting of individual log cabins, and I rented one by the month. An electric water pot and skillet met all my cooking needs. I even baked an upside down pineapple cake. Once, I decided to fast on water and honey with one tablespoon of honey at each meal. I felt so clean and had more time to spend in the Word. It would be so simple never to have to eat, but.... on the seventh day hunger returned.

In the 'fifties, in order to travel to Payson you had to take a long ride from Globe with the mailman. On that one-lane dirt road, hugging the mountains, the dear mailman drove faster than was safe, around the curves, for the thrill of it and to test you to see if you could make the grade from being a city slicker to being a mountaineer! I made it! And I told him it was only because the good Lord was on my side. He did not want to hear about the Lord but entertained me with hairy tales about Superstition Mountains, about Billy the Kid and that "thar's still gold in them thar hills."

After my summer in Payson, on my return trip, the same mailman took his sweet time at the café. This meant that, according to his schedule, I would miss the Greyhound in Globe. However when I arrived, the bus was at the station, and the bus driver was standing at the open door. He asked, "Where are you going, lady?"

"To Los Angeles."

"I was just standing around and waiting for you. Hop in!" was his playful remark.

"Lord, that was You again!"

In the Los Angeles area I met several people interested in my dowsing. Among them was a preacher who took me to his gold mine in Nevada. I outlined the direction of the vein and pointed out where he should dig. A year later I asked him about it: "That was a very good lead you gave us!" he said in an important tone of voice telling me he had made a good strike, yet he never offered even a token of the profits. I did not expect such a raw deal from such a man.

This same preacher had interested me in the study of our American Christian heritage. Earlier, I had been studying the prophecies, from Daniel to Revelation, and their historical fulfillment. That opened a window on the Great Tribulation, on the Rapture, on Babylon the Great. One subject lead to another. They were biblical and they were right, but they replaced my intimate fellowship with the Lord. Instead, I became carried away on the wings of history, pushing aside the inner Voice.

Much of the next three years were spent studying the endless genealogies and the whereabouts of the Ten Lost Tribes of Israel. It was fascinating, but Paul warned Timothy not to give heed to fables and endless genealogies, which minister questions rather than godly edifying, which is in faith. I wanted to go my own way and do my own thing. He let me.

Some other people from Los Angeles wanted my help in Nevada to stake out claims. There was a cabin in a ghost town where I could live, and the landlord was more than happy to let me have it rent free so it would be occupied. The original room had been built by a Swiss miner and was in prime shape. Life was very primitive and restful, no electricity, no running water. I spent my time reading and writing when not attending to my needs, and visiting with the few families living in some of the shacks. The people I helped came on weekends from Los Angeles to work on the claims. They brought food and supplies, meeting my needs. Someone brought me a handgun; I promptly sold it. The Lord is my shield and my defense. Most men carried a gun and murders were not infrequent.

At the Post Office, I met a woman who invited me to her house in the wooded hills. On Sundays, her husband was a deacon in a little church in Bishop, California. The rest of the week he was mining with a helper. When I came, he asked if I would show him which way to dig in his shaft. My dowsing rod was always with me. I obliged. Three months later I asked about his mining. "Oh," he said, "we dug out eighty thousand dollars from the vein you showed us."

"What did you do with the money," I asked.

"We sank it back into the hole!"

What? Again I received no payment of thanks. "Don't those people have a conscience? A sense of obligation?" I asked myself. Apparently not; however, neither the preacher nor the deacon asked for my help again. Some One must have bothered them about their unrighteousness.

Nevertheless, when the deacon's well dried up, I offered to dowse for water. A hundred feet from the house I sensed a good reaction and showed him and his helper where to dig. The water should be at thirty-seven feet. "Impossible," was his response, "there is a granite ledge at that depth."

"I don't care. There is water at thirty-seven feet."

I met him the following month and inquired about the well. They had dug to thirty-seven feet. There was no water. Tired and disgusted, they had come up leaving the motor, the jackhammer, and other tools at the bottom of the shaft. A couple of days later, deciding to go back to mining, they went to recover their equipment. It was deep under water. Yet, I hardly received a thank you. Slowly, and painfully, I was learning my lessons.

It was 1963, and I was still in Nevada. One morning, a neighbor asked me to come with her to Tonopah to shop. We stopped at the hotel for a cup of coffee. A bunch of men were watching television. Suddenly there was a big commotion on the screen and a deep gasp from the audience. "The president has been shot!" We all watched the ghastly scene unfolding before our bewildered eyes. We left the hotel. On the street, no one knew what had just transpired.

I cannot forget that date, November 22, 1963. It was also my forty-eighth birthday. Awestruck, I inquired of the Lord, in spite of my backslidden condition. "Why did You permit this?" Deep within, I could see that America was making John F. Kennedy a national idol. Indeed, there was hardly a home or a business that did not display his picture. I had noticed some placing flowers by these pictures, making him almost an object of worship. God could not allow that. We are a nation under God, and He is a jealous God. In God must be our trust. It is not a coincidence that this occurrence remained shrouded in mystery.

This event stopped me in my tracks. Where was I going? I was now interested in all kinds of things, while my Bible remained on the shelf. I had been backsliding, falling into temptation and sin. The world around me was collapsing. My gold venture did not work in spite of my good and true intentions to mine gold to finance the Proclamation and spread of the Kingdom of God. The Lord did not need my gold, for the Kingdom is not built with corruptible things like silver or gold, as Peter says.

With the oncoming spring I finally came to the end of myself and cried out to the Lord in repentance. I had ended up on a pile of ashes, as Job had. I had to admit that I had become very self-righteous, thinking that nothing evil could happen to me. I had to be humbled. "Forgive me Lord." I kept singing: "Although You slay me, I know that my Redeemer liveth!" I began fasting and repenting and singing: "*I know that my Redeemer liveth*!" I kept persisting in my repentance even after the Lord spoke: "You are asking for a hard thing." I was frightened; had I sinned against the Holy Spirit? But I kept trusting in His infinite love and far-reaching mercy until I felt the warmth of forgiveness. My intimate relationship with the Lord was restored, and I was willing to go back to California.

There was something else bothering me, namely my dowsing. It was too daring and too close to the realm where evil powers could take over the rod. I was using latent soul powers I knew too little about, and I gave up dowsing—I knew the Lord asked me to stop it.

Because water was a matter of life in the desert, and as I had found water for a family that otherwise would have had to move away, I was free to ask them to take me and my belongings to Lancaster, at their convenience. Meanwhile an official from the ghost town of Goldfield told me of their poor water supply and asked me to help them with my dowsing rod. Their last well was drying up. "Lord, may I dowse just once more. These people need water." I felt free to help, and located what I sensed would be a good supply. The men started to dig right away. The well was still quite shallow, when to everyone's delight water started gushing and turned into a small geyser. The official came running to give me the good news. What a blessing this was to a couple of hundred desert folks.

"Thank You, Lord, for leaving this generous gift behind."

26

Reality

One Dream Collapsed; Another Came True

After Nevada and some collapsed dreams, I settled in Lancaster, California, where I resumed caring for the needy in their homes. This time it was not by word of mouth recommendations, but through the Employment Office. Welfare paid for my services, and I saved the money for close to two years. This was enough for a down payment on a lovely house in Tehachapi. The purpose of the house was to give a home for wayward girls, the kind I cared for in Girls' Town. According to news reports there was a need for foster homes, and with my previous experiences, I thought I qualified. I had an interview with the social workers in Bakersfield. Everything seemed to be working well. The need was great, and I should hear from the department within a couple of weeks.

I was telling the Lord what I wanted to do for Him and prayed for His blessings. I quit my job in Lancaster and went to prepare the home to receive four girls. Then I waited. I waited for two months. Finally I called the social worker, inquiring why I had not heard from them. "Because we have no problem girls." "How can that be?" I asked myself. "No wayward girls in all of Kern County?" Then a letter came advising me that I did not qualify after all, because I had no personal income and should not count on the girls' welfare money to cover my personal needs and that, presently, they had no girls to place! Only God could have set up such a situation.

As another dream collapsed, I became desperate, "Lord, Why? Why did it not work? I will hang unto Your coattails and not let You go until You tell me what goes on in my life and what it is I am doing wrong." Every morning I walked around the garden and bothered the Lord to speak to me. In the evening, as it became my custom, I sang to Him and read His Word.

Day after day for three weeks I did not let go. My cupboards were getting empty. I ate the food supplies prepared for the girls. Money was also running out, but the only thing that mattered was an answer from the Lord. I persevered until one afternoon a flash of light came down to me from heaven, accompanied by a sense of elation. I knew it was from the Lord. I took my Bible and continued reading in Nehemiah, being particularly interested in the names of the twelve gates. They seemed to indicate spiritual experiences: the sheep gate— salvation, the water gate— baptism, the fish gate— testimony, etc. I had to look up the meaning of the Miphkad gate. It meant an appointed place near the altar where sin offerings were burned. "Lord, You died for my sins. The only thing for me to do is to "*present my body a living sacrifice, holy, acceptable unto God which is my reasonable service.*" I read on until I came to the prison gate and visualized Nehemiah standing outside of the city with companies of people, of mighty men, of rulers, all giving thanks, all prepared to open the gate and enter in.

A thick veil dropped from my spiritual eyes. God was inside the wall! My wall! I was holding Him prisoner! Nehemiah and his mighty men were singing and praising and giving thanks and then opening the gate to enter into the city, Jerusalem! It was my turn to open the prison door that held my Savior bound.

I saw that within me were two sets of wills, minds, and emotions, one set belonging to me and the other to God. As I read the Word, I would receive revelations from the Lord, but I made a big mistake in that I would put into action these revelations without checking first with the present will of the Lord.

Yes, He was a Person within me with His will, His mind and His loving emotions, *but,* what could I or anyone else do for God? I learned that I had to subject my own will, mind, and emotion to God's. I had to know His will and His mind for my personal life, to obey Him and trust. By myself, I could not succeed and by His mercy, He would not allow me to succeed.

The vision was clear. Christ was in me and I had to submit my will to His, my thought and desires to His. For this *I* had to get out of the picture. I was very eager to die to myself, but I had to see that even *that* dying could only be done by the Lord. This was made clear to me one night. I was dreaming that I laid in a coffin on the dining room table (a European habit of laying the dead in state for three days before burial). One of my legs stretched outside the coffin. As I was putting it in, the other arm fell out. I was wiggling and could not lay still. I started laughing and woke up. "You cannot make yourself dead. I will do it for you! Indeed you cannot even crucify yourself. You have no way to drive in the last nail." The Word says: "*Deny yourself,*" not crucify yourself. The *denying* is the death to our self, to our soul.

One thing was clear: To let the Lord direct my life consciously, I had to get out of the way! I had a very strong sense to burn all my old photos and a large painting of myself done by a talented painter in New York. All vestige of my past was gone. All I kept were my naturalization papers and a couple of other identity documents.

A further testing of my heart came. Would I leave my own ways behind? I felt it was being ground to pulp, and I recognized that in going my way I was prone to deception and failure. I confessed some more and gave up. "Lord, you are right; your ways are right because only You know what is the best for me." In my repentance my heart was bleeding. I was embracing the cross, and simultaneously His love was flooding my being, and I was being healed.

Better than ever before I saw that the Lord demanded unconditional surrender. At the time of my ignorance God winked, but now He commanded all men (me) to repent (Acts 17). Through subsequent years, I found strength in maintaining a bleeding heart, in embracing the cross, thus reaping inexplicable joy!

This was a tremendous and a deeper direction in my life: from an outward leading, choice and environment to an inward speaking. It made me check with the Lord on every detail of my life. I no longer needed to take chances on my own "good will tours"! Now I had the mind of the Lord and His will at a moment's notice; however, there still remained a learning process on how to recognize them.

A Dream Come True

My new direction was to give up the house to the bankers and respond to a call from a doctor in Mojave to nurse one of his patients for a period of two to three months. My loss of the house was an infinitesimal price to pay for the spiritual light received.

My prayer was to be holy as You are holy, to be perfect as You are perfect! For this, I knew I had to die to self. I needed the Lord. On Sundays I attended a little church in Mojave. The pastor was preaching: "We are under grace, not under law!" That sounded strange: don't we have to keep the law? It took me some time and a better knowledge of the Word to comprehend: we do have a better law, the law of the Spirit of life, the law in Matthew 5, 6, and 7.

Galatians was a new discovery, and I spent time in Romans 6,7, and 8. Indeed I was a wretched man, but there was a new life in me—Christ in me the hope of glory! With Christ there was another law, the law of the Spirit of life. I was experiencing a little flicker of reality.

One verse was coming back to my mind over and over: "*That I may know Him, and the power of His resurrection, and the fellowship of His sufferings, being made conformable unto His death.*" Mostly I wanted to know the power of His resurrection. It was not the power of the Holy Ghost preached by the Pentecostals. I knew that much. But no preacher would or could preach on it. I was eager to know it, to experience it. I wanted the reality of the power of resurrection. No one ever spoke of reality. Yet the real God was the One I knew.

At that same time, Psalm 87 became my aspiration: "*His foundation is in the holy mountains. The Lord loves the gates of Zion more than all the dwellings of Jacob. Glorious things are spoken of it, the City of God. Selah. I will make mention...this man was BORN there. Of Zion it shall be said, this and that man was BORN in her: and the Highest Himself shall establish her. The Lord shall count, when he writes up the people, that this man was BORN there...*" No one preached on it, and although my mind did not quite comprehend, my inner being responded, for this also corresponded to the verse of my salvation: "*You are come unto mount Zion, unto the city of the living God, the heavenly Jerusalem...*"

What was this all about? Someone explain! I desired the reality of it. In another small, independent congregation I overheard an octogenarian named William, and his wife Rhonda, sharing on reality. My ears immediately pricked up at that word. I approached him and his wife to tell them that *reality* is what I was looking for and that I was seeking fellowship with like-minded people. They lived in Morongo Valley and invited me to come by faith. This sounded so good. I had a clear sense to go, and I agreed to come as soon as my patient went home. Their son would come for me and my belongings.

My thirst for true fellowship was drawing me to this couple. I wanted to drink from the well of their experiences. We had daily Bible study, prayer and singing, as the Lord led. This was something I had yearned for. It was a dream come true. Most of our study pertained to inner life, "*Christ in us the hope of glory....in Him dwells the fullness of the Godhead bodily and we are complete in Him... Eat Me and you shall live by me."* The words of the old prophet near Riverside were coming to pass! I was eating of the Head, of Christ. Although I could not explain nor expound on it then, we enjoyed coming together, reading and believing. "*Faith comes by hearing, and hearing by the Word of God.*" It was real!

As soon as I arrived in Morongo, I found a one-room house with kitchen and bath and a job caring for a stroke patient under the direction of a physical therapist. I felt at home in this beautiful and friendly desert. Everything was at walking distance and people were so welcoming, not just to other people, but to desert life as well. We all kept a pile of kitchen scraps and leftovers a few feet from the house where we could observe the desert fauna come for food. There were chipmunks, squirrels, road runners, rabbits, quails and, late at dusk, coyotes. Their orderly schedule was impressive. No one intruded on the other, and everyone was tucked away safely in their respective habitat before the oncoming coyotes.

Everything was perfect, a dream. I was immersed in a deep peace—no striving, no struggling. I testified freely of the reality of Christ, particularly among my "patients." My gift of healing was often coming through my hands as I was giving a massage. Having heard of my work, an elderly Jewish man asked for some treatments. He had a private health spa with a jacuzzi attached to his home. As I was massaging him, I testified of our living God and Christ, the Messiah. "I envy your belief, but I simply cannot believe in God." What a sad conclusion to such a long life, and I was not skillful enough to put faith into him. When it came to settle with me, he asked, "How much?" I answered that I did not charge but left it to him and his heart. "But I do not have a heart. You are out of luck."

"Then give me the minimum others give, $5." He did not ask for me again. God makes those who refuse Him very uncomfortable. At this juncture let me mention another old man I met walking his dog.

"You have a beautiful dog," said I to start.

"Yes, he is my best friend. Dogs are better than people."

"But they do not know God."

"I do not believe in God. Once I die, that is it."

"You mean to say you are content to die like a dog? What about the life after?"

"There is no life after. My dog dies; I die like him. They'll just put my old carcass into the ground. That's all."

We parted. What sad, sad endings. What horrid outcome they will face at the Judgment Day.

I had to take the cleansing blood over such experiences, so that the Lord could have the freedom to speak. He asked me to give Him my mind, to trust Him to think for me. "How could I do that? I would lose my identity. I have already given you my will and my heart." His answer came, "Trust Me. I'll do the thinking for you." At another time He said that I did not need to try to develop more independence; on the contrary, Christians should depend on one another. And, speaking of rewards, He said, "*I come and My reward is with Me*." His presence was my ample reward.

During those days I experienced much inward adjustment. From childhood on, fear and apprehension would come when I heard my name called. "What have I done now?" was my immediate reaction. I was led to read a book on cybernetics of the mind and its feedback. This was a tremendous help on understanding the working of my shattered nervous system and of what more needed to be healed. "Lord, do come in before my reactions because they are so fast I cannot stop them." This was my prayer then, as it is still now. For it is a lifetime work, touching our disposition. At least I overcame all apprehension when someone would call my name.

Thinking that I had arrived, spiritually speaking, I wanted to remain in that blissful state forever, but the Lord had much more in store for me. My Morongo experience was merely a Selah, a pause in the wilderness by the oasis of Elim and the seventy palm trees, where I camped by the waters.

What a fellowship, what a joy divine,
Leaning on the Everlasting Arms!
What a blessedness, what a peace is mine,
Leaning on the Everlasting Arms!

Leaning, leaning,
Safe and secure from all alarms;
Leaning, leaning,
Leaning on the Everlasting Arms![3]

27

KLAMATH FALLS & VICTORIA, CANADA

Klamath Falls

Through my stroke patient, who was in a wheel chair, I was introduced to a Christian club of invalids in Riverside, most of whom were in wheelchairs, and to their attendants, who called themselves the "Good Sports." We had prayer, fellowship, sharing of our experiences, and some games. Often we "Good Sports" went to cheer up the handicapped, but in reality we were the ones being cheered up, fed, and blessed.

One of the attending nurses, Louise, insisted that I move closer and live with her in a quaint apartment attached to her house. My inner sense said, "Go." Before moving, I made sure there was a proper replacement for my services in Morongo valley. Because of the weakness of our eighty-year old friend, William, our Bible studies were discontinued.

My stay with Louise was very brief. Through a dreamlike vision, the call came to go to Klamath Falls, Oregon, and contact a widow there. Louise understood and stored my belongings. It was a warm California fall, but winter was on the way in Oregon. Someone gave me a beautiful fur coat saying, "It will be cold up there!" How considerate our Lord is!

A "Good Sport" attendant drove me to the bus station where there was a four hour wait. What should I do? I considered out loud, "How about visiting Paul, a naval officer from the Pacific wars and a member of the invalid club?"

"Good idea. I'll take you to him," said the attendant.

My last quarter, yes, twenty-five cents, went for the storage of my suitcase.

Paul and I had a sweet time of fellowship in the Word. When he asked about my plans, he also wanted to know if I had any money to go to Klamath Falls. "No. The Lord must provide; He is sending me." To expect a gift from an invalid did not even occur to me.

"How much is the bus fare? And you will need some cash for the first week until you find your way." He wrote me a generous check and called his bank four blocks away, so he could introduce me and make sure that they would cash my check. How thoughtful our Lord is!

In Klamath Falls, I attended services in a mission that gave asylum to a number of "hoboes," homeless men who would ride the freight trains, stopping at missions for a few days for food and shelter, then moving on to another train, another destination. Klamath Falls was an important crossroads, with trains rolling every which way. The men had their pick of places to go. Some of the men relied on their lucky stars. We tried to tell them that they had a heavenly Guide to rely upon, the Lord Jesus Himself.

During one of the services, I was prompted by the Lord to share of His great love and His marvelous salvation; however, when I looked at the dismal crowd, ill-kept and unshaven, I turned away. I was offended by the outward look of these men, and I didn't have the boldness to speak. Then I realized that actually I was empty of the Lord's love for all men, and so I walked out of that meeting. For an hour I dealt with the Lord, acknowledging my lack of love, my lack of belief that He died for them also, and I acknowledged my desperate need for Him. I was so ashamed. By the time I returned to the services, they were over and the chapel was empty. The Lord continued to bother me about this all week.

By the following Sunday, His love could finally flow through me to these *misérables* who lived constantly under condemnation. They did not need to hear more about hell and damnation; they lived in it. They needed to hear about Jesus, about His redeeming love, about His merciful forgiveness and powerful salvation. They needed to know that there was another life!

I shared, standing from my seat. As I sat down, a preacher on the platform stood up with his hellfire and brimstone sermon. I looked him straight in the eye, turned around, and walked out the full length of the central aisle. I was hopeful that the man understood my disapproval of his condemnation, but I doubted it. I was blessed to have seen something shining in the men's eyes after I had spoken. I had experienced a little more of "how loving and how just our Lord is."

Rescue the perishing, care for the dying.
Jesus is merciful, Jesus will save![4]

Victoria, Canada: No Room in the Inn

Klamath Falls turned out to be a stop-over on an extensive journey. While in Klamath Falls I had a definite awareness, through a dream where I "saw" a bus, its destination "VICTORIA." I knew then that the Lord was sending me to Victoria, and I simply had to go. Along the way, in a bus, I again "saw" in a vision a little, white, country church with a steeple, among large downtown buildings. I knew no one in Victoria and had only sixty cents in my wallet. "I will test your faith," said the Voice.

On the ferry crossing from Port Angeles, Washington to Victoria, I inquired about the white church and asked if someone could direct me to such a building. "Oh, yes," said a man. "It is very close to the port." He gave simple directions. Passing by a small hotel, I asked the clerk to kindly keep my suitcase while I looked around town.

I found the little white church by a city park. All the doors were closed. "Lord, what do I do now?" I sat on a bench and started to read the Bible.

"You are too religious," came the Voice, "Go and meet people." Some gardeners were working by the side of the park, mixing manure.

"I see you are digging for gold!" We laughed.

"Yes, it is for the lawns of the bowling greens," said a newcomer. "Have you bowled before?"

"No. I have not seen this game in the States, but I know it is an English pastime."

"Come. I'll teach you how." He was the owner. I was terrible at it, but the man was very kind and obliging.

During the ferry crossing, I had studied a map of Victoria and its surroundings. The little settlement of Esquimault caught my attention and seemed to be my destination. I asked my new bowling partner how to get there.

"Very simple," he said. "I'll show you where to catch the bus. It'll cost you fifty cents, but meanwhile, let's have lunch, for it is noontime." He did not take me to a fast food restaurant, but to a fine vegetarian restaurant! After the meal, we parted company.

"How well You do all things, Lord!" I retrieved my suitcase and paid my bus fare. Once more, the single dime left over might be needed for a phone call.

The bus did not quite reach Esquimault. "Lord, I am not losing heart; I must go on." At the corner pharmacy I asked whether they knew of any active Christians. Yes, there was a church up the street. It was open; the pastor and wife greeted me. I told them of my dilemma and that I needed a ride because the Lord had sent me to Esquimault. "You are lucky. We are normally not here weekday afternoons. Give us a little time to finish our work, and we will take you." I waited patiently most of the afternoon. Finally, we got into the car, and I was asked about the address.

I didn't have an address and so I answered, "Stay on the main road. I will tell you when to stop." I was not anxious but very alert.

I was thinking inwardly, "Lord, how will I know?" We kept on driving.

"How much further is it?" asked the driver. His tone of voice changed and he sounded aggravated. That was my clue.

"Please, let me off at the intersection right ahead, and I am so thankful for your service. The Lord bless you."

"Here I am, alone in the woods. You taught me to be practical first and to keep my feet on the ground; now, therefore, I need a place for the night," I told my unseen Pilot. There was a small grocery store at the street corner. There were usually bulletin boards in such stores that often advertised rooms for rent, but here there was nothing. I asked for the local newspaper. It was sold out. I voiced my need to the store cashier. A customer overheard me and invited me to look in the newspaper at her house, next door to the store.

She insisted on carrying my suitcase. I introduced myself as a missionary. My mission was Jesus. I was asked to wait a moment in the living room. By the books lying around, I could tell she was a Jehovah's Witness. It did not matter. I had learned to overlook such denominational differences, and not to inquire about people's affiliations, but only to share Christ. Neither did she inquire about my beliefs.

Soon she called me from the kitchen. To my amazement she had prepared a meal for me, because it was suppertime she said, but she would eat later with her husband.

"*Take no thought for your life, what you shall eat...for your heavenly Father knows that you have need of these things.*"

In the newspaper there was a room for rent. This dear lady called and made an appointment with the man for seven that evening. Meanwhile, I could leave my suitcase with her. The room for rent was above the fire station, a ten-minute walk. I enjoyed a beautiful stroll on the path strewn with pine needles, under majestic trees. Then I climbed the old steps to a dingy, poorly lit hall. I knocked at the indicated door. There was no answer. I waited a few minutes. No one came. Across the hall a door was ajar. As I came closer the woman inside saw me. "Has the landlord come?" I asked.

"No, but come and sit down."

The room was as dreary as the hall. There was a bare bulb dangling from the ceiling, an old couch, and an oil stove. In the background was a kitchenette with a little table and two chairs. So sad! But not as heart-gripping as the woman's expression. I forgot all about my needs and let her talk. She opened to me. I spoke of the infinite compassion and love of Jesus and of the comfort He alone can give.

This was Simone. She had come from eastern Canada to separate herself from a drunken and abusive husband. Her job as a cleaning woman paid minimum wages. To help out, her thirteen-year-old son distributed papers. We prayed. She felt consoled. I promised to return after I found a room.

When my Jehovah's Witness host learned that I was still homeless, she had a suggestion, "There are nuns in an estate close to the fire station. Go to them and ask them for hospitality. After all, they are supposed to help the stranger and the wayfarer!" To retrace my steps and walk beyond was nothing, but psychologically I had to surmount a mountain of emotions which had been in control up to now. First of all, it was humiliating; second, and even worse, I had not liked nuns since my childhood. Whenever I saw one on the sidewalk, I would cross to the other side. Yes, there was a root of bitterness in my heart, and I was put in a situation where I had to recognize it, overcome my bitterness, and forgive the nuns for my orphanage years.

After I rang the doorbell of a stately and impressive mansion, I waited, then rang again. There was no response. The nuns had to be there. I walked around the well kept and well lit grounds until finally the door opened and three nuns, representing three generations, stood there, their curiosity obviously piqued. I felt relaxed and at peace. All bitterness had left.

Introducing myself as a missionary, I told them that I needed a place to spend the night, not having the means to take a motel room. I said I would gladly repay by doing some work in their adjoining convalescent home. The middle-aged nun quickly and coldly denied my request, saying that I should find a motel. Peeking in, I could see a large drawing room with several couches good enough to sleep on.

"What will you do?" the older one asked, expressing some concern.

"I do not know; but one thing I do know: The Lord promised never to leave us nor forsake us. He has a way. Thank you." As I walked away, I remembered Bethlehem: *"No room in the inn."*

It was a balmy summer night. "Lord, I am not an orchid. I can wait out the dawn under a tree, but it is only eight o'clock, and I have time to revisit Simone to cheer her some more." She was happy to see me. There was a faint smile on her ravaged face, and her son was with her. The Lord was the subject of our conversation, and an hour went by quickly, after which I excused myself, ready to leave.

"Have you found a room?"

"No, not yet."

"It is too late to be walking around. Stay with us."

Incredible! There was room in this tiny inn where actually there was no room. Indeed, it is a matter of the heart. Here were open hearts!

"Simone, you are too kind. Where will we all sleep?"

"Behind you, there is a bedroom for you. Michael and I will sleep on the couch. The back reclines. We have done it before," she insisted. The double bed occupied most of the bedroom, leaving just enough space for a dresser and room to walk around. The communal bathroom was in the hall.

The Lord had admonished me to go from open heart to open heart, by faith and not by sight. “Tomorrow,” said Simone, “I’ll go to work, and Michael to school. Help yourself to all the food you want. There is soup in the refrigerator. Make yourself at home as long as you need to.” What a heartwarming end to a very long day!

To be brief, I stayed three days and unabashedly ate the food she offered, trusting the Lord to supply. On leaving, I asked Him to bless this woman and boldly told her that I was leaving the blessings of Elijah behind me because of her unselfish giving. The following year I visited her in a cheerful two-bedroom cottage under the pines. Her spiritual and financial condition had greatly improved. Michael was happy too, painting his bedroom. Thank you, Lord. You do all things well!

During the three days I had stayed with Simone, I had walked about the sparsely-populated, wooded area and had come across a small church with what seemed to be a pastor’s house. I knocked at the door; the man was home. I told him of my mission and offered my services to the sick and the poor. I asked whether anyone needed help in his congregation. He thought for a while.

“Oh, yes. An elderly man in his eighties lost his wife lately and needs help with cooking. Let me talk to him. Come tomorrow, Sunday, for the service. I’ll let you know then.” The following afternoon I met Edward.

Edward lived in a large and comfortable house trailer. He gave me the master bedroom, happy to have me stay and do some cooking, read the newspaper to him, and help with his mail. I was surprised to find that he was illiterate. His wife had taken care of all the written matters during their long lives. Edward was a barber, a good one. He had worked only in the barber shops of the finest hotels in Canada and had done well. His wife had kept all of the accounts. After retiring, they had been able to live comfortably.

With her passing away, however, Edward was at a loss. How can one live so long and not learn how to read? I was puzzled.

Upon observing him, I came to connect ignorance to pride. Edward was not incapable, it was just that he had been too proud to learn. Some people are just like this, always covering up for their lack of knowledge, and therefore, depriving themselves of the chance to learn.

Edward was five feet five inches tall, slender, standing erect and proud, reminding you of a little rooster, always ready to assert himself. Otherwise, he was kind and pleasant. I was glad to assist the dear man. We helped one another. I also had plenty of time to myself to contact people for the Lord.

Only believe, Only believe
All things are possible,
Only believe.[5]

28

Phyllis

I met Phyllis on the first Sunday in Esquimault when I had been asked to give my testimony. I said, "Jesus is real!" It was received with some reservation, with the exception of one woman who came up to me after with her face beaming:

"You are an answer to prayer. The Lord sent you just for me. Would you come and share our dinner in my humble home?"

Phyllis was in her mid-thirties, living with her nine children, ages four through sixteen, often trusting God for their food because the husband was an alcoholic who spent too much of his salary on booze. He was a frustrated engineer, too proud to accept any help. But when he could no longer pay the rent, he was forced to accept Phyllis' father's offer to live in his summer cabin by the lake. The one-room cabin had a large table, several chairs, and a couple of benches. The kitchenette was in a window alcove, and another alcove contained a built-in double bed with an improvised bunk on top, for the youngest boy. The other four boys slept in the garage. The four girls slept on boxes in the basement on the dirt floor. The wet walls, spiders, and mosquitoes did not seem to bother them as they were tucked in by their loving mother who daily committed their young lives to the Lord, their loving Father.

Phyllis had a living faith and a close contact with Jesus, whom she trusted implicitly for the care and safety of her children. She would say, “Lord, I give them the best care in the house, but once they are out of my sight, it is up to You. I trust You to take charge.” She had to be very resourceful and happy, strengthened by the joy of the Lord in order to keep a close-knit brood of children satisfied and close to home. I marveled at her.

Her most difficult task was probably the laundry. She did have an old washing machine with a wringer in the basement. The problem was in drying the clothes in very damp and often rainy weather. Clotheslines were strung through the house, anywhere possible, and a wood fire was kept burning.

The cabin was a skip and a jump from the “rain forest.” There was a magic about that forest. Everything was green: the leaves, the ferns, and the moss. Everything was living, every branch or tree trunk covered with moss. Lush ferns concealed the ground. Raindrops lingered on the leaves, and a mysterious mist enveloped the whole, even on days when the sun's rays tried to peep through the forest to the ground. You had the sense of penetrating the sacred territory of trees. Spontaneously, the hush overcame you, interrupted only by the gurgling of a brook.

Trees create their own atmosphere. The giant redwoods in California control the humidity and temperature under their green umbrellas. Once, visiting a redwood park near San Francisco, I saw a two-thousand-year-old tree growing out of another tree that was two thousand years older! The older tree lying in the brook was petrified. The minerals of the water flowing through the trunk remained deposited in it, changing its nature to stone.

Think about it! The living tree started to grow when Jesus walked the earth. The petrified one grew from the time of Abraham through the Old Testament to the New Testament age. What a tremendous witness! I was impressed.

Phyllis and I spent most afternoons together with our Bibles, and often in the quiet of the “rain forest.” Dear Phyllis, she was a seeker and not satisfied with organized religion. She wanted more. She was very happy when I told her that the Lord did not come to give us religion, but life and life more abundantly, until rivers of living water flow from our bellies! Although I did not quite understand it, yet something was stirring in me just to speak this Word. Jesus said that He was the way, the truth, and the life, not the dead letter, not formal doctrines and teachings that kill.

I shared with her my wanderings in the jungles of endless denominations, gleaning glimpses of truth here and there. From the very beginning of my conversion when sitting in front of a community church in Palm Springs, the Inner Voice spoke: "You may attend but not join." Then I came to the book of Revelation where the Voice from heaven said, "*Come out of her (Babylon), my people.*" I realized that my stand was justified and that I was not a black sheep after all; however, I still was not clear about the Kingdom of God.

Through the centuries, Bible scholars have identified the Catholic Church as the Great Babylon and the denominational churches as her daughters. I came out of "her" thanks to my built-in Treasure! I met not a few seeking ones who had also come out. Some were meeting in free groups; others remained alone with no place to go, being silently prepared as living stones, waiting for the day of the fullness of times when God will gather in one all things in Christ. "*They that wait upon the Lord shall renew their strength. They shall mount up on wings as an eagle.*"

"Helena," said Phyllis, "you have opened my eyes. I can carry on even after you leave. The Word is so real! Jesus is real!"

The Hidden Man of the Heart

Many opportunities presented themselves to witness for Christ. No one was a stranger to me. To strike up a conversation was easy, and it easily turned to the Gospel. On one of those self-initiated occasions I met an English lady from Victoria. She invited me for tea at the Empress Hotel. Neither of us drank

English tea. She ordered "silver tea." The tingling sound aroused my curiosity. The waiter brought a pot of hot water and cream. She mixed cream and sugar into her cup of hot water. "That is it! Try it; it's quite good." (Really, it was better than one would imagine!) The occasion was only a distraction, a setting for sharing our experiences of Christ, on following the inner sense, the Person of Christ within us. For us to live is Christ!

The English lady said, "There is a small book in our library you must read. There is time to fetch it before the library closes." The booklet, written by Bishop Allen of the Anglican Church in the late twenties or early thirties, contained no more than fifty pages. It was full of enlightening pages that illuminated my inner being, showing me what had happened in Tehachapi when God explained that His Personality was in me!

The title of the book, *The Hidden Man of the Heart*, corresponded to my experiences. God was in me, in my heart. The Treasure planted in my heart had a desire, a will. He had His own thoughts and desires which I had to contact and obey. The book attracted my attention to Mary, who magnified the Lord in her soul and in her spirit rejoiced over God her Savior. Besides her soul with her personality, Mary had a spirit. I pondered that. Here, the spirit was separated from the soul. It was something else! Like most others, I thought that the soul and spirit were the same. But to make his point clearer, the Bishop quoted First Thessalonians 5:23: "*And the very God of peace sanctify you wholly; and I pray God your whole spirit and soul and body be preserved blameless unto the coming of our Lord Jesus Christ.*"

My spirit was definitely one thing, my soul another, and my body a third. No wonder nothing worked for ten years in my initiating programs to please God and meet His needs through my soul, myself. I kept considering: if my personality is in the soul (everyone knows that), then God's personality was in my spirit! Something satisfying was transpiring in my inner being; however, my mind could barely hold the revelation, and the thought was fleeting.

I laid the booklet aside, needing time to reflect and let this truth settle in me. It was tiring me out. When I picked up my reading again and touched on Romans chapters six, seven, and eight, more light came. Actually, I had experiences in all three of these chapters. I now received the explanations and could relate to the Word. This was my hidden manna. Although I had no skills to share the revelation with others, the Bible became a new book to me.

Still, I was groping like a three week-old kitten with eyes partially closed, but I kept on reading: "*Walk after the Spirit*" in Romans; "*Walk in spirit*" in Galatians; "*Walk in Him*" in Colossians! I had been walking by listening to the inner Voice; now I found out that the Voice was in my spirit, that the Spirit dwells in my spirit, not only in my heart! It was a most ethereal thought! I let the matter rest. Trust and obey was still my motto. I could distinguish the Lord's speaking. For the time being, at least, it was enough.

Trust and obey,
For there's no other way
To be happy in Jesus,
But to trust and obey.[6]

29

Preparations

One morning, the Spirit's speaking came loud and clear: "You will go to Europe several times. I will use you. Prepare to leave." February just began; six blessed months had elapsed since my arrival in Victoria and Esquimault. I did not doubt nor question how the finances would come. I set out by first advising Ed and Phyllis. "The Lord wants me to move on. He is sending me to Europe!" Their hearts were prepared; there was no sadness.

Ed offered to pay my way to Seattle and took me to the bus station. Another acquaintance asked me to deliver a personal message to someone there who gave me room and board and more cash. I applied for my passport and picked it up twenty-four hours later—a super fast process. From Seattle, I went back to Klamath Falls and to the widow, who was genuinely happy to receive me. She invited others to hear of my spiritual experiences in Canada; they in turn supplied my needs and sent me off to California. I left my fur coat, so helpful in Canada, with the widow, encouraging her to wear it.

In California I visited Louise, who was keeping a few of my things, and Paul in the wheelchair. Paul was always interested in my adventures in the Lord.

And so, step by step, giving my testimony of the Christ in me, our hope of glory, I moved on from open heart to open heart, receiving donations without ever asking for a penny. The Lord was putting it on the hearts of the people to give. My adventures in God kept multiplying. His ways were always different. This time He was sending me from one person to the next like a package! A package of experiences in God! How I loved adventure stories in my youth! These experiences surpassed them all because I was living them, not only reading about them.

However, for years I had not been free to tell of my experience of being slain, then being saved, nor of the Almighty speaking to me. I skipped that part of my testimony, partly because I did not thoroughly understand it. I did not understand, for example, the analogy to the worm, until I read in Isaiah: "*Fear not, thou worm Jacob*," whose name was changed to Israel meaning "a Prince of God!" Nor did I understand the meaning of why I had been headed toward destruction until I realized that I had been looking for God in the physical realm and trying to bring Him down to my level. The sphere of God is only in the Spirit. "*God is Spirit, and those who worship Him must worship Him in Spirit and truth.*" None of my research had been pleasing to God because I searched in the realm of my mind. Nicodemus, a Pharisee and ruler of the Jews, did not know this either. He came to Jesus to be taught. Jesus replied, "*Marvel not that I say to you, you must be born again...that which is born of the flesh is flesh, and that which is born of the Spirit is spirit.*"

Before my conversion, the Lord allowed me to search and discard one thing after another so that I could prove and convince myself that God was not in all of those man-conceived cultures and activities, nor in the mental inventions of religion and philosophy. Then, when I was out on a limb, having discarded all but man himself, mercy and compassion reached me. A flow of rich experiences followed.

One of these experiences was quite unusual. At a summer camp in Tennessee where I was invited to share, I received an invitation from a pastor who had his own independent church in Detroit. All the people I contacted on this trip had left organized religion. The pastor from Detroit invited me to come to Detroit and speak to his congregation. On leaving, he said, "Call us when you arrive in Detroit; we will pick you up." When I came to buy my ticket however, the flight was booked up. Only first-class seats were available.

"Lord, what do I do now?"

"You told me you wanted to serve me first-class" (when I was in the seminary). What a sense of humor! I carefully counted my cash. Of course the Lord planned exactly what I should have. There was ten cents left! Again! That was to give me a sense of security, humanly speaking, in case I needed to make a phone call.

The Anointing

The pastor and wife greeted me cordially and took me to their home. At the prayer meeting I was introduced, and some asked for special prayer and counseling. So far so good. I could trust my inner self. But when the announcement was made that I was to give the message on Sunday, I was frightened. The pastor was an accomplished speaker. The congregation was spiritually well-disciplined. For the past three years they had been studying the book of Ephesians, while I was still in verse 1:10: "*God will gather together in one all things in Christ.*"

On Saturday, I hid in my room most of the day to be alone with the Lord: "You know I cannot preach, and You are not giving me a message!" I was desperate; the Lord was silent. Agonizing, I sat on the platform the next day. Agonizing and empty, I came to the pulpit facing some hundred and fifty faces shining, alert, and full of expectation.

"Let us all pray!" Everyone prayed in loud voices, and then my directive came: "Open up to Isaiah!" I said. I started reading and asked the congregation to read after me. At times we prayed about what we read, and so, on and on. As we touched on the reality of the Word, the anointing came, and the presence of the Lord was so strong that within a short time praises took over. Some witnessed the presence of angels; others were healed, and prayers were answered. This was not only unusual; it was extraordinary, even miraculous.

Three women who had asked to see me after the service came to inform me that my counseling was no longer needed. Their requests had been answered! I received gifts, flowers, money. People were making someone important out of me. I suppressed a sense of self-glory. "No, Lord, I had nothing to do with this flow of blessing; this was all strictly from You!" Now I could see and understand how some evangelists become spoiled and carried away by pride. I did not want to be in such a position, knowing it would spoil me for good. The Lord heard my cry and closed the door to such ministry. I see it was a test. Thank God, I passed it.

Why had I not received a message before I spoke? Maybe because the Lord wanted to do something spontaneous through an empty vessel, to show, maybe to the preacher, that He did not need man's eloquence. Through my agonizing, life could flow. "*So then death works in us, but life in you.*"

The Christians I had been meeting during this extensive journey were outside of religion. We were seeking, searching, knowing only that there was more and that we had not yet arrived. With Paul we could say: "*Not that we have already attained, but we pursue.*" I was pursuing the Kingdom of God! No one, yet, had given me a satisfactory answer as to what and where this Kingdom was.

Reading Ephesians in a more careful way, I began to wonder about the body of Christ. Paul says it is the church. What church? Some preachers preached on the body of Christ as referring only to the apostles, prophets, evangelists, shepherds and teachers, practicing what they called the "Body Ministry." I could not accept that. My Treasure, and my spirit were not agreeing.

From Detroit I was recommended to a believer in Chattanooga who in turn sent me to Washington, D.C. "You must meet sister Doris. She has an accounting office and is hard to see, this being income tax return time. But I'll call ahead to tell her of your coming." Doris had very little time indeed.

"Sorry, I am so rushed, but the Lord told me to give you this." She opened her Bible to a hundred dollar bill, to help me to my next stopover, which was New York.

Where He leads me I will follow,
Where He leads me I will follow,
Follow, Follow all the way![7]

30

Europe

In less than four weeks I had covered much ground since leaving Victoria, and I had many spiritual experiences. Now the ultimate question was, who would finance my trip to Europe and whom was I to contact? I must not lose sight of my ultimate destination.

After three nights in a small hotel, my money was gone. The Lord was silent. The only vague impression I had was that of a man in black. Who and where was he? I was distressed as never before, and in my despair I remembered Boris, my mother's cousin, with whom I stayed in 1939. I called him and he came immediately. This was of the Lord; He wanted me to contact my family. Boris still lived in the same apartment overlooking the Hudson and the Washington Bridge. His wife and sister-in-law had passed away. Of course, he was lonely and insisted I stay with him. Boris was kind and generous with me. He was the man in black.

Now that I was settled, I could formulate my plans. The *U.S.S. Constitution* was leaving New York harbor for Le Havre, France, the first of April. From where would the money come? I told Boris of my plans to take the ocean liner and visit our cousins in Southern France. He knew that I did not have the means. I assured him that I believed it would come.

I had three weeks to spend in New York, and I visited my friend Georgette in her posh business salon on Madison Avenue. We had not seen each other nor corresponded in fifteen years, not since my Greenwich Village days, and not since my conversion. She could not comprehend my giving up the business, nor my life style, nor why I had wrecked my life when I could have been a millionaire by now, had I kept my retail business. What could I say! I let her talk.

"What are you doing right now?" she asked. She needed someone to take the inventory. Would I do the job?

"I will do it gladly. I have time on my hands." It was a tall request, for she wanted one accounting sheet displaying the stock on hand and an entire month of entries of purchases, sales, and returns, and gifts, etc., at a glance.

How well I remember walking up and down Riverside Drive talking to the Lord about the problem. "How would You do it, Lord?" The idea came: Use different colors to identify the transactions. Put two of the largest available accounting sheets side by side to record every day of the month on the horizontal lines, and the stock on the vertical lines. Wonderful. I was happy and executed the project. The Madison Avenue accountant was so impressed that he asked to meet me and suggested Georgette keep me. My salary would be the same as it had been fifteen years before when I was working on Madison Avenue! "Sorry, Georgette. I must move on. I'd rather keep you as my friend."

During my three weeks in New York I also visited Bible bookstores, looking for literature along the order of Bishop Allen's *The Hidden Man of the Heart*. No one seemed to know what I was talking about. Then, at the Christian Missionary Alliance bookroom, I found a book with an intriguing title: *The Release of the Spirit* by Watchman Nee. It quoted some of the same verses used by Bishop Allen, and as I read on with anticipation, I could relate to some of the words. I bought the book and kept reading it in the evenings. However, much of it was unclear then.

Europe was a dark spot on the horizon of my memories. Recalling the hard times, the dire poverty and death of my beautiful and talented mother, disturbed me. I never liked to think about the past. The Lord came in to quiet me down and reassure me that my trip would be in resurrection and that I would find a new Europe. My apprehensions were dispelled.

Usually, Boris and I would eat supper together. He would bring some food "to go" and some caviar for a treat. After supper, I read the Bible to him in Russian with great difficulty, for lack of practice. Time was marching on. Sunday night, March the twenty-fourth, Boris asked if I had received any money. "No, not yet." I was not anxious.

"Do you still want to leave next week, April First?"

"Yes, of course, I want to get on that ocean liner."

"Helena, I am deeply indebted to your family. As a young student in Russia I spent all my vacations at your family's estates free, accepting their hospitality. I would like to repay some of it by helping you. Meet me at my bank during my lunch hour. We will take out some money for your fare."

"Lord, You are an extraordinary accountant!"

His bank was across the street from Rockefeller Center and from a travel agency. Calm and composed, we crossed over with a thousand dollars in twenty-dollar bills. Why in twenties? Only the teller knows. The travel agent could not control her look of surprise when I asked her to book me on the *Constitution* leaving the following week. Having made a few phone calls, she secured me a cabin for four, the only one available. She apologized because it was too late to print my name on the passenger list and to receive the other insignificant favors. What amazed her was our matter-of-fact attitude and our assurance that there would be room.

"Most people book weeks, even months, ahead in much excitement and anticipation. After all, this is a very special occasion, and you are so cool!" she said.

I booked the return trip by plane. To the Lord in me, this was just another step—although a long one.

During the crossing, the weather was wonderful, although cool. Oh yes! Georgette gave me a sporty mink coat she no longer used. Paris can be quite cold in April even after the chestnut trees start blooming. When I set foot in Le Havre on what should have been solid ground, it was in motion. I had not been sick on the sea; now I became ground-sick! I took a taxi and asked the driver to find me a small family-like hotel.

"Le Patron" at the desk got angry with me because occasionally I would slow down in my speaking, trying to recall a word. "What's the matter? Can't you talk?"

"Sorry. I have not spoken French in thirty-two years. I forgot."

"How can you forget French?" He was typical! Big on pride, short on temper.

Le Havre during World War II was razed to the ground, bombed out. Now, following the reconstruction, it lacked the old country charm. Large and cold perspectives, gray monuments in commemoration of the war dead, statues to unknown soldiers, wide avenues flanked by ugly box-like cement buildings two to three stories high—the view was impersonal.

I went for a walk to recover my ground legs and find a little restaurant. When "Le Patron" brought the fish soup I had ordered, I looked at it in disgust. It was a thick, darkish gray mess. Should I try it? I did! And what a delightful surprise. The taste was inexplicably delicious. The French really know how to cook. I went shopping and bought a French Bible. I needed to learn the biblical language. The next day, I took a train to Paris and stopped at a hotel recommended by a passenger.

My Cousins

Boris had supplied me with the addresses of cousins (the older generation had passed away), including that of Anne-Marie, the daughter of Madame Bour, our patron during my college years. I called her and was invited to spend a few days with her. She lived alone in her mother's huge apartment overlooking the "New Trocadero"; the old one had been torn down. Anne-Marie was very open to me and my testimony.

"There is a nun I want you to meet. You speak the same language. Be sure to stay with me on your way back from the south; meanwhile I'll tell her about you and make an appointment. She is very busy and hard to get a hold of."

In remembrance of old days, I went browsing in the "Quartier Latin," the "Student District of the Sorbonne." They were rioting, as before! Life had not changed much. Anne-Marie took me to the farmers' market and we stopped at the bistro for coffee and croissants, a typical French breakfast. At home she prepared the most scrumptious "Coquilles St. Jacques," a seafood baked and served in large sea shells. Evenings, she worked on a tapestry in "petits points" and I knitted. The atmosphere was very congenial and harmonious.

At the train station on my way to Marseilles, the porter asked me, "Who are you?"

"I am an ambassador of Christ!" was my answer.

"Madame, you look it!"

Of the five cousins with whom I had ridden the donkeys around the Basilica of St. Sofia in Constantinople, and with whom I had frequent contact in Paris, I planned to see only four, as the fifth one was in Germany. I had not seen them in thirty-two years and was eager to meet them.

First, I contacted Michael at his work in a travel agency downtown. He was very cold and told me to take the streetcar to his apartment. His wife was there. "Thank you very much," I said. That was a blow! I took a taxi. The wife was indifferent. I stayed a day or two, long enough to find a way to Olga. Olga, the one that used to give me nightmares, was married to a bankrupt aristocrat—no children. She rebuilt a half-in ruin farmhouse of her husband's family and grew roses that kept multiplying and spreading over a quarter of an acre. Her sister Tatiana, who was my friend back on their farm, was unhappily married to a medical doctor by whom she had two children. They lived in Villeneuve near Avignon and the famous Palace of the Black Popes who had split away from Rome.

From Avignon, I returned to Marseilles to visit with Nina, who was kinder in her reception of me. None of these cousins had much contact with one another—their common denominator being frustration! We had nothing in common; none was interested in God. I was appalled at their lack of heart and clung to the Lord.

"Lord Jesus, but for your infinite mercy, your love and your choosing me, I would be in that same pathetic situation without God and without hope. Thank you for letting me see where I came from. I cannot be grateful enough! Lord, make me more appreciative of my new life."

France in May of '68 was in political and economic turmoil. Strikes encompassed all means of transportation on land and in the air, with both public and private transportation being affected since the oil refineries were closed. Nina lived in Marseilles, and my plane back home was to leave from Paris, a thousand kilometers away. I still had ten days, but the strike promised to be of long duration. On one of my walks downtown, and through some nasty demonstrations, I came to a travel bureau. In front was a big commotion around a bus driver and his old bus.

"We are leaving for Paris in three hours!" he shouted. Then he looked at me. "Do you want to go? You'd better make up your mind right now while seats are available." He was rough, but I sensed the Lord's beckoning. I bought my ticket. Three hours gave me enough time to pack and return. Nina was very surprised. I took advantage of the situation to tell her how the Lord was my Shepherd and was making a way where there was no way.

As she accompanied me to the bus, we were curious to know where the gasoline had come from since the refineries were on strike. We found out! Two enterprising bus drivers near the Italian border crossed over and bought a supply of gasoline, enough to drive to Marseilles, pick up a load of passengers, and drive to Paris. The men *du Midi,* from southern France, are a special kind: entertaining and very jovial. They are hot and quick tempered. The trip promised to be interesting.

Both drivers sat on a double seat, and as one drove, the other rested or joked. There was no need to stop the bus to change drivers. The one who drove simply stood up holding the wheel while the other slipped into his seat from the back then took over the gas pedal and the wheel, all without skipping a beat. They were experts. We left in the afternoon with their promise to arrive in Paris in the morning, nonstop. Of course we did stop for a delectable dinner near Lyon and some quick restroom stops, except that there were no restrooms. "Get out if you need to. Gentlemen to the left; ladies to the right. Relieve yourselves in the night." French people are very nonchalant about those matters. We made the trip on good roads and in record time. After all, there was no traffic.

Paris was paralyzed and empty, but again the Lord had a way to take me to Anne-Marie, by a hotel limousine. It was like a homecoming. I did need my heart warmed up after the previous disappointments with my cousins. We spent a good sweet time together and visited the aged nun she had mentioned. The convent was a very fine building. We came to a large entry with a spiral stairway. A young nun met us and asked us to wait in the drawing room. Soon we heard young footsteps bouncing lightly down the stairs. Anne-Marie looked up and whispered, "There she comes, You would never guess that she is in her seventies!"

Indeed, the nun was a bundle of joy, contagious. We greeted one another as longtime friends in the joy and love of the Lord. We found "*the One whom our soul loves.... His love is better than wine....He is altogether lovely...!*" (Song of Songs).

Then she said, "I am so happy that you are free. Your place is to be in the world but not of it, while my place is here. You might think that I should leave the convent, but I must stay to minister to the young nuns and set them free." Our visit was like a refreshing breeze.

This nun was well known in France for being instrumental in cutting the long convent garb to street length and in replacing the headgear by a less ostentatious kind. Inwardly, she was preparing the nuns for the coming Bridegroom! What a blessed encounter this was. Anne-Marie delighted in listening to our conversation.

The strike was still in progress when my time came to leave. The airports were still closed. "The Lord will make a way," I told Anne-Marie. The Americans are very resourceful and prepared. I called the agency. Yes, we were leaving tomorrow they told me, and they said that I should come to the agency, which was actually at walking distance to where I could board a limousine. A friend helped carry my luggage. I traveled light. We parted with a prick of sadness in our heart. I never saw Anne-Marie again. The Lord took her a year later. Amen.

We were driven to an improvised army airstrip barely long and wide enough for a jet. We were parked in a vegetable patch waiting for the take-off, among peas and beets and beans. All went smoothly.

He holds the whole wide world
In His Hands,
He holds the whole wide world
In His Hands,
He holds the whole world in His Hands[8]

31

Sons of God

On my return to the States, there was no need to stop in New York. Georgette was busy, and as to Boris, I had discovered that he drank at night. At times he would walk up and down the corridor at two or three in the morning, very agitated. I felt uncomfortable as it had become worse towards the end of my first stay. It was better not to go back, I thought.

From the airport I went directly to Penn Station to take a train to Washington, D.C. I had a little time and went to the bookstore, where I had previously bought another Bible and *The Release of the Spirit,* to see what else I could find by Watchman Nee. To my joy there was a book entitled *The Song of Songs*. Was it a coincidence? No. The nun and I had been fellowshipping about *The Song of Songs* in Paris. Now the Lord wanted me to understand the message of the Song. I lived with that book close to a year, reading a verse with the expounding paragraph almost daily. Through it, I had a year of honeymoon with the Lord.

Before going on with my travels, I must retrace my spiritual steps. I had to buy another Thompson Reference Bible because some pages of the old book were marked up, used up, even torn. The edges were frayed; the gold edging was gone. The worst pages were in Romans 6, 7, and 8, the books of Galatians, Ephesians, Philippians, and Colossians, and in the book of

Revelation 1, 2, 3, 20, 21, and 22. Those were my favorites because of my need to better understand the law of the Spirit of Life, the Spirit of sonship, Christ making his home in my heart, the Overcomers, the end of the dragon, and the New Jerusalem.

These verses were like delectable, mysterious, attracting pieces of a big puzzle. No one preached on what I could sense in my spirit. But at least two books were of great spiritual help: *The Hidden Man of the Heart* by Bishop Allen and *The Release of the Spirit* by Watchman Nee. Watchman Nee explained in more detail than Bishop Allen what this inner man, this new life, was all about and what was going on inside of me. However, I was perplexed by words like *breaking of the outer man* and *releasing of the spirit.* His vocabulary sounded strange to me, and I did not understand it all at first. However, I knew that Christ was making His home in my heart and that I was to walk by Him, by the Spirit.

Over the past three years, Romans 8 had been becoming real. I had met one brother in Los Angeles (we started calling one another brothers and sisters in the Pentecostal movement) who spoke on sonship, saying we are not adopted sons but real sons. "*The Spirit itself beareth witness with our spirit that we are the children of God: and if children then heirs; heirs of God and joint-heirs with Christ*" (Rom. 8:16). "*Christ in us, the hope of glory*" (Col. 1:27). Hallelujah!

This brother had told me about a group calling themselves the "Sons of God" who met on an estate in Maryland. "Stop in," he said, "when you have the opportunity. No invitations are required. Your new birth is your passport." I had stored this information within me, and now, returning from Europe, a sense came to visit the "Sons of God."

The estate was easily reached from the Washington train station by bus. There was a constant flow of brothers and sisters on the spacious grounds. People were coming and going from many states, preaching, teaching, fellowshipping; we were sons, we were the overcomers, we were the manchild of Revelation 12.

It sounded so good, but subconsciously I felt something was missing. Where was the woman that brought forth? Where was the church? Was it the church of the Firstborn? No one ever spoke about her. Certainly *I* was not going to start it.

Again, by His infinite mercy I received a dreamlike vision in which I saw the remains of a chimney left from a house that had burned down. The hearthstone of the chimney was a perfect cube of translucent and shimmering silver. In my dream I asked the brothers with me to lift it up because the key to our quest was inside. No one would, at first. Finally one brother took the stone and the key inside rattled. My inner Voice spoke, "What you are looking for is on the west coast." I woke up.

This could only be interpreted spiritually. Starting with the hearthstone, which is the headstone of the vault of a chimney, I was reminded of the Stone rejected by the builders which became the head of the corner: Christ. A perfect cube of silver indicated the silver that stands for the price of redemption. Christ is the Redeemer who bought the church at a great price. Thus the chimney signified the church. Within the hearthstone, Christ, was the key to all our quests.

The house, representing organized Christianity built up by the efforts and labor of men, was as wood, hay, and stubble. It had to burn down. Only the center of God's House, the part built with stone, remained. Christ still had a witness on earth of which He was the cornerstone, the Head. "*I will build my church,*" He said—not the pope, not the cardinals, not the bishops, nor the reverends.

Small as it is, His testimony has survived through the ages, from the time that Christ as the rock started laying the foundation, the first stone being Peter. The stone chimney of my dream stood high above the ashes of burned down religion. I had to go and find it somewhere on the west coast.

The next morning a sister on the estate asked me whether I would accompany her to Tulsa because she did not want to drive alone. Doors were opening quickly. We stopped at a gas station to service the car.

"You won't make it around the corner in this thing," said the attendant. The warning had the effect of a drop of water on a hot pan. It evaporated. Nothing natural could quench our spirits. We went around the corner and then twelve hundred more miles on heavenly praises and Hallelujahs!

The secret to keeping the car going was to keep the ignition on when refueling; otherwise, the motor would not start. However, since it was overheating, we had to stop the motor a few times. That meant that we had to sit and wait for it to cool. The weather, fluctuating between ninety and ninety-five degrees, was not conducive to a cooling process during the day. Thus we Hallelujah-ed our way to Tulsa, Oklahoma. "Lord, surely you were our chauffeur and our engine!"

In Tulsa, I visited the offices of a prominent evangelist. A huge portrait of the evangelist met you at the entrance—and in every subsequent room. The place was obviously his work, his domain, and his small monarchy. The impression was that of a prosperous business. I was disappointed.

The sister arranged for a ride to California for me, with a couple. Overnight we stopped with a family near the gorgeous town of Sonora, Arizona. On my walk, I came across a private airfield high on a plateau. The only man around was working on his plane. I greeted him and commented on how impressive the beauty of the view was.

"Have you been to the end of the runway?"

"No."

"Let me give you a ride in my jeep."

Here the view was truly spectacular, even breathtaking. Towering before us were the three most famous rocks of Arizona: the Bell, the Church, and the Court. To me, they represented liberty, worship, and righteousness.

My Lord spoke to me, "I will build my church from the ground up." The rocks made me understand that it would be a grassroots operation, that is, something which would grow out of the hearts of people, and not out of an organization.

My dream gave me some direction. I had to pursue this new treasure hunt. At least I knew I had a destination: the west coast. The expanse did not concern me, having gone on treasure hunts with the Lord before, not even knowing what I was looking for, such as in Victoria and Esquimault, where I found Phyllis, a real gem. This time I needed to find brothers and sisters who could give me some answers and put the pieces of my puzzle together.

"Seek and you shall find!"

32

Fear Not

When I arrived back in California, I retraced a number of my steps of the previous years, starting with a visit to Louise. Doors opened to visit groups of friends with whom I shared the Word. As to my vision, I kept silent but on the alert, listening for spiritual clues to give me further guidance. "*Fear not, little flock, it is the Father's good pleasure to give you the Kingdom.*"

I was still looking for the kingdom on earth. Yes, I knew that the kingdom of heaven is within us, that the kingdom is righteousness, peace, and joy in the Holy Spirit, and that I had experienced peace and joy, even exuberant joy at times. But I was alone, and I wanted a visible expression of this reality with others.

"Lord, where are those who have the same yearning?" I visualized that as we live a holy life individually and with others we would express the kingdom on earth. "*Thy Kingdom come, thy will be done on earth as it is in heaven.*" I saw this, and I believed it; it was my hope to find it!

There was no particular leading. I went from open heart to open heart, from San Diego all the way to Klamath Falls. It was a heart-warming experience. These were my sisters and brothers and were so much closer to me than my own biological family.

In Klamath Falls, the same widow received me again joyfully. We went to different free groups together, and my inner sense kept nudging me to go on to Victoria. I picked up the fur coat that had been stored for me and went on.

Ed, the octogenarian I had helped, had moved from his trailer to a small house, and I found him painting it. "Let me help you. I like to paint," I said. He invited me to stay with him at least until his brother came from eastern Canada. I accepted; however, Phyllis was the one to whom the Lord had sent me. We were like two peas in a pod, two sisters in the Lord, in His love.

Since I had started to read the *Song of Songs* by Watchman Nee, I was elated and full of joy. I had received the "*oil of joy for mourning*," and, "*in His presence is fullness of joy*." My joy was full. I could hardly contain it, and it spilled over to Phyllis. We had such a blessed time together, almost daily for a couple of months. When Ed's brother came, she asked me to come to her modest dwelling and stay a while longer with her and her family. Of course, the only place for me to sleep was in the basement with the girls. "Lord, if it's good enough for them, it's good enough for me!" Neither the dampness of the walls nor the spiders with their cobwebs bothered us.

The girls happily made my bed on boxes, and we had a slumber party. I told them how much the Lord loved them and that we can love Him as our heavenly Father. He likes us to talk to Him, to pray to Him, and to tell Him our needs. I said that we should ask Him for some beds and yarn and knitting needles! I told them we can make a list of our needs and check them off as our prayers are answered. The girls prayed for a bed and knitting needles. Everything came the very next day! A neighbor brought a nice bed with bedding. The girls insisted it was for me. I had to accept, but on my one condition. The two oldest had to learn to knit, and I would teach them. Later, a double bed came for the girls.

The boys were cold in the garage. "Why don't you boys pray and also tell your heavenly Father your needs?" They prayed for a stove. The following day a friend of the family came by.

"You boys need a stove?"

"Yea!" they applauded.

The friend brought an oil stove in his pick-up, with a fifty-five gallon drum of oil. "The stove does not heat without fuel," said he, giving the boys a pat on the back. They installed it themselves. The children's faith rose three hundred percent and so did their prayers. God was real! Reality is what I wanted them to touch.

Food gifts were coming from one source or another the whole time I was there. My heavenly Father made sure I was no burden on the family finances. How can you not rejoice with our God and love Him? Phyllis, reassured that God was her partner in bringing up the children, did not mind my leaving her again. I returned to Klamath Falls.

My dear widow welcomed me, wanting to hear further testimonies. Jesus was on my lips. I kept speaking to individuals, to home groups, to anyone that wanted prayer, and my needs were met. I was not a bit concerned. My budget was kept in heaven, and I had the best Accountant. I cannot even recall how most of my needs were supplied that year. My income had been below seven hundred dollars a year, for several years, yet I was lacking nothing, wanting nothing. "The Lord is my Shepherd, I shall not want!"

In serving others spiritually and physically all these years, I was served, and often humbled. On one particular occasion a sister brought a beautiful black suit of fine wool with exquisite detail; it even had a silk satin lining. "I bought this for you for five dollars at the Salvation Army Store."

"Where?"

At first I felt a piercing dagger, piercing my pride and cutting it off, right then and there. "It's all right, Helena. I buy a lot of my clothes there. Come. Try on the jacket." How could I resist her? I put it on. It was a perfect fit. Even the sleeves were long enough. I am on the tall side and have long arms. This elegant suit opened the door to my clothes shopping. What a relief! It was affordable and so simple. Whenever there was a need, I went to the second hand stores to see what the Lord had prepared for me!

As to my transportation I remembered the deal I had made with the Lord: I would keep speaking and He would keep supplying the rides. Fifteen years had elapsed. I had forgotten about it, but He had not. As I testified, He kept me on wheels, on planes, and on boats!

One afternoon, sitting on a rock overlooking the city of Klamath Falls, I said, "Lord, in Luke You said that it is the Father's good pleasure to give us the Kingdom. You told me that what I was looking for was on the west coast. Lord, where are You building? I am tired of prophecies, and I know too well what Satan is doing, but how about You? Where are You building?" My only sense was to keep on going. "Not that I have already attained, but I pursue," said Paul. "Draw me and we will run after you," said the Song of Songs. Brother Nee wrote that the drawing power of the Lord Jesus Christ Himself generates the pursuing power in us.

I kept pursuing and laying hold of the hope set before me, "which hope I have as an anchor of the soul both sure and steadfast." Outwardly it seemed that I was homeless and aimless, but inwardly my roots were in the heavenlies, for my hope had entered within the veil.

My hope is built on nothing less
Than Jesus' blood and righteousness.
I dare not trust the sweetest frame,

But wholly lean on Jesus' name.
On Christ the solid rock I stand.
All other ground is sinking sand!
All other ground is sinking sand![9]

I'm pressing on the upward way,
New heights I'm gaining every day.
Still praying as I onward bound,
Lord, plant my feet on higher ground.
Lord, lift me up and let me stand,
By faith on Canaan's tableland.
A higher plane than I have found,
Lord, plant my feet on higher ground![10]

Year after year these hymns were a sweet melody in my heart, as I went from one experience to the next.

33

Home, Sweet Home

Caring for the Sick and the Dead

Making my way down through California, I stopped in Lancaster, where I had worked before, to help a young woman care for her two young children while she went to the hospital to deliver a third child. During the couple of weeks that I was with them, I was told that the Convalescent Hospital needed a person to distribute medication and that I should apply for the job, as I was known to be careful and responsible. I would work next to the director of nurses and under her supervision.

I sensed it was the Lord's provision, and I remained in Lancaster several months caring for the sick. This constant traveling with its varied activities had a very beneficial effect on my character. The Lord would not let me settle on my lees nor be satisfied with my latest revelation or experience from the Spirit. He always carried me on further, molding my character, washing out undesirable traits.

One of my peculiar traits was a repulsion of people's feet and an unusual repugnance of seeing a dead person. Was this sense of repulsion a feedback from my orphanage days when we seldom bathed and the smell of dirty feet would turn my stomach? And were my experiences of dead corpses lying on the street during the Russian Revolution still bothering my subconscious mind? At any rate, I did not want to come near a corpse. Yet, one morning at the Convalescent Hospital, upon entering a women's ward on my medicine route, the patients immediately informed me that the lady in bed number three had died. I went to her and took her hand in a most normal way. She was still a little warm. "Let us wash her up, comb her hair, and dress her for the coroner," I told a nurse's helper.

That was not even my responsibility. I did it in a matter-of-fact way. Everything came so naturally, as if I had been trained for the job. Later on in life I even studied foot reflexology. All repulsion and repugnance were gone. "Lord," I asked, "when did You work these traits out from my character? You are amazing!"

One time I found an older male patient perturbed and overcome by fear. "I am going to die! I am going to die!"

"Bernie," I said, "you love the Lord. Don't be afraid. For you to die is a release. You will be happy when the Lord takes you. Commit to Him your spirit, as the Lord committed His Spirit to the Father on the cross." He calmed down. I could not remain since I had to finish my medication route, but I asked a Christian worker whom I met in the hall to go and comfort Bernie.

The following week I found Bernie sitting up in bed, beaming. The room was effervescent with the presence of angels. "They are coming for me; the angels are coming for me!" Bernie was exuberant.

"Yes, I know. I can tell. The room seems full of them."

Later that afternoon Bernie was gone. Humanly speaking, one could be sad, but spiritually one should only rejoice. What a joy to depart in the Lord! It reminded me of my Grandfather Schwachheim.

The head nurse often suffered from intense headaches. I offered to give her a massage to relieve her pain time and again. She spoke of it to the doctor in charge of the clinic and the hospital next door. When he saw me he asked, "What is this I hear about you? Do you want to work in physical therapy? Our therapist needs a helper."

"Sure," I replied.

In the physical therapy department, I quickly developed a good reputation: "Go and see Helena. She is fabulous!" I only did my job, prayed, and witnessed when proper to do so, unaware of my hidden gifts manifested by my Healer behind the scenes. Once more, He did the work, and I received the credit. However, the job did not last. My therapist became ill and someone else took over the department and let me go a month later, in spite of the fact that the doctor had said, "Helena comes with the department."

"In all your ways acknowledge Me, and I will direct your paths."

Caring for the Living

I sensed from the Lord that I was needed back in Morongo Valley and later in San Clemente. In Morongo, Rhonda, the widow of the octogenarian who recently had passed away, needed comfort. They had been so closely knit in the Lord that she literally lost her other half and passed on shortly after. Many Christians visited her, and one of them spoke of a body of Christians living together. They lived close to one another in Los Angeles, near Vermont Avenue, not in a commune, but in the same neighborhood. My interest was aroused. For years, I had been looking for Christians who had the same aspirations and spiritual goals. I expected Christians to live together, like in a kingdom, but the Lord was silent.

Our fellowship with Rhonda and with others was deep and satisfying. At times we felt immersed as if into a spiritual substance. It was so thick one could cut it with a knife, to use a common expression. The words of the Bible were real; we were eating them and experiencing the reality of Jesus being the bread of life. "*Eat me and you shall live by me.*" Unfortunately, when the inner stirring was so strong that I thought I could not contain more, I would turn away. Yet, surely the Lord wanted to give me more of Himself.

When I revisited my former stroke patient in the wheelchair, her son, who came for the day, invited me to spend a week at his home in San Clemente. This was a second invitation, the first one having come from a teenager, Marianne, who loved the Lord. Our paths had crossed a few months before in San Francisco.

I called Marianne as soon as I arrived and went to her house at the invitation of her mother who wanted to see me. I found the mother distraught because of an uproar in town caused by a Christian Bible Club, of teenagers. Marianne belonged to them. Their leader had brought them into a high pitch of excitement. Nothing else mattered but Jesus and the Bible. True, but they became very insubordinate at home as well as at school.

The dear mother was almost in tears. "We are Christians. We read the Bible, but we also lead an orderly life. Marianne is eighteen, my oldest. She was my right hand helping with her four siblings. Now she has no time for her responsibilities at home. At school, the teachers are upset because the club members read the Bible during classes and forfeit their homework. Is that proper in your eyes?" she asked.

"Of course not! What would you like me to do?"

She asked me to fellowship with her daughter and boyfriend. I agreed to, but only in her presence and that of another adult.

My fellowship was over the numerous biblical examples of obedience and subordination. Starting with the return of the boy Jesus from the temple, I continued by reminding the young people of the fifth commandment, to honor their parents, honor meaning respect and obedience. Paul in Ephesians speaks of submission to one another and he exhorts children to obey their parents in the Lord, for this is right. To Timothy, Paul wrote that children should be in subjection to the household, with gravity. In the book of Romans, an entire chapter is dedicated to subjection to authority, to governments, "*for the powers that be are ordained by God.*" School teachers are ordained by God. The

Scriptures had a sobering effect on the two young people, and the word was passed around. Marianne's mother was very thankful. My job for the Lord was done.

My week in San Clemente was up, and the obvious thing to do was to return to Morongo Valley. However, while coming to the Lord through His Word and continuing my reading in Revelation 3, I received a strong speaking through verses 1 and 2: "*I know thy works, that thou hast a name that thou livest, and art dead. Be watchful and strengthen the things which remain, that are ready to die for I have not found thy works perfect before the Father.*" I sensed the Lord saying to me, "Go to the people who live together."

This word shocked me and hurt me. Yet the Lord also gave me a way of hope, "Go to the people." I also wanted to know why my works were not found "perfect" or "fulfilled" (Greek Interlinear). Was it because I was a loner? But I was not a loner by choice. From the very beginning of my new walk in life, at the seminary, I was looking for people, Christians, who lived together in God's Kingdom. In fifteen years I had not come across them, and I belonged nowhere! Yet I was not losing hope. I was enduring, driven by my spirit to keep on seeking.

Among the free groups, I found a number of godly persons who thought like me. We felt we were stones cut and shaped for the building, just like the stones for the temple in Solomon's days. Those were cut at the quarry and then brought to Jerusalem to be polished and fitted into the temple. First Kings 6:7 reads, "*The house when it was in building, built of stone made ready before it was brought thither: so that there was neither hammer nor ax nor any tool of iron heard in the house while it was in building.*"

Ephesians 1:10 continued to encourage me: "*When in the fullness of time He might gather together in one all things in Christ.*" A few months before, in Klamath Falls, I had asked, "Lord, where are you building? In Maryland You directed me to the west coast. Are You now sending me to the people who can put my pieces of the puzzle together? Could those people be the stones of the chimney in my vision? All I know about them is that they meet near Vermont Avenue."

The fact that this avenue was about twenty miles long did not disturb me. I had followed leadings before not knowing where I was going. The Lord would guide me. I purposed to go. So, instead of returning to Morongo Valley, I decided to first stop in Anaheim to share with my friend Bea the latest speaking I had received. Immediately a ride was provided.

Bea and I had met in Anaheim the previous year, 1968. She had come out of the denominations. We were reading the biography of Madame Guyon. When Bea, with other Christians, opened a house for newly converted drug addicts on Webster Avenue in Anaheim, I went to minister Christ and help rehabilitate these new believers. Some still suffered from withdrawal pains. We gave them all the help we could. I even moved in for a short time. Most of the young people were in their teens and early twenties. They bounced back within a month and were able to go back to school or work. Our concern was for their spiritual life. Where would they go after leaving the Webster home where they had had a daily rich Bible study and plenty of hymn singing? Bea and I earnestly prayed for what I called "a spiritual clinic" to give proper nourishment and guidance to misguided youth.

Now that the Lord had said that my works were not perfected before the Father, I went to see Bea to tell her about my new experience and of the shock I felt having received such a severe speaking. I had been satisfied, thinking that I was reaching my purpose by helping others, and by leading people to Christ. I thought I was living, yet I was dead and did not know it. Seemingly, I was also satisfying the Lord and the Spirit, yet my works were not found perfect before *the Father*. Obviously, there was a deeper step to take, a step to satisfy *the Father* and *His* purpose. I did not know what this purpose was. I only knew His guidance in my personal life. As to *His* purpose, my mind was blank; however I was given a new direction: "Go and meet those people who live together." There was hope ahead.

"Bea," I said, "let us go and find out about those people." At that very time, one of the former drug users, Jay, came for a visit. "I know where it is," Jay said and gave us directions.

We went there to a meeting. Five of our former drug users welcomed Bea and myself with open arms. It was comforting and rewarding to see that these young people had gone on to seek the Lord. They had found the place before we did! The meeting hall was very plain, the chairs were arranged in a square. Some two hundred brothers and sisters, in casual clothes, were seated facing each other. At first, nothing impressed me. They sang wholeheartedly as in many other groups. Only when the speaking began did I become truly excited. The sharing was on the spirit, soul, and body, using the same verse of First Thessalonians which Bishop Allen and Watchman Nee had expounded, "*I pray God your whole spirit and soul and body be preserved blameless unto the coming of our Lord Jesus Christ.*" The ones sharing at this gathering spoke on the Body of Christ, and on the reality of the Kingdom in this age and on its manifestation in the millennium. These people were truly caring for the living!

That evening at the meeting, I received some of the answers I had been looking for. I was also offered hospitality. Bea returned home to Anaheim. That night, the Lord awoke me from a deep sleep and tapped me on my right shoulder saying, "You belong to this flock."

Previously, I was always so free and independent, now to be part of a flock would be a restraint. "Lord—this will restrain me!'

"I submitted to restraint!" said the Lord. In a flash I saw Him as a babe, and jumped out of bed to stand at attention, saluting, "Aye, Aye, Sir!" I went back to bed as a great peace flooded my being.

After all my yearning, searching, and travels, at last I felt that I belonged. My sense was that this small group of genuine seekers who knew what I had known in my heart, was the church of His choice, and not the church of my choice! Previous to this

I had a collection of spiritual puzzle pieces that I didn't seem to be able to fit together. Now, some of the delectable pieces of the puzzle started to fall into place, such as the meaning of the power of resurrection, of the reality of an inward life, of Zion and of the New Jerusalem! For the first time in my life I had the sense of belonging. I was finally home! The Treasure in my heart had brought me home.

The verse received at my conversion began to come to light:

"*Ye are come unto mount Zion, and unto the city of the living God, the heavenly Jerusalem, and to an innumerable company of angels, to just men made perfect, to the church of the First Born,*" (Hebrews 12:22). With Isaiah, I could "*Cry out and shout, ye inhabitants of Zion for great is the holy one in the midst of thee.*"

Surely goodness and mercy shall follow me
All the days, all the days of my life;
And I shall dwell in the house of the Lord forever,
And I shall feast at the table spread for me.
Surely goodness and mercy shall follow me
All the days, all the days of my life.

Endnotes

[1] Isaac Watts
[2] Walter Chalmers Smith
[3] Elisha Hoffman
[4] Fanny Crosby
[5] Paul Fader
[6] John H. Sammis
[7] From a Pentacostal Meeting
[8] Negro Spiritual
[9] Edward Mote
[10] Johnson Oatman

To order additional copies of

THE TREASURE IN MY HEART

send $15.00 (price includes shipping and handling) to:

Helena Schwachheim
1255 S. Nutwood #6
Anaheim, CA 92804